"**Fashion** IS THE **Mirror** OF **History.**"
—ATTRIBUTED TO LOUIS XIV

WHY'D THEY WEAR THAT?

Sarah Albee

FOREWORD BY **Tim Gunn**
OF *PROJECT RUNWAY*

NATIONAL
GEOGRAPHIC
WASHINGTON, D.C.

CONTENTS

Clockwise from upper left: ancient Egyptians, about 1400 B.C.; Japanese samurai mask; baths, ancient Rome; Queen Elizabeth I, 1588.

Clockwise from upper left: an 18th-century version of a very fashionable angel; the bicycle craze, 1895; mini-skirt, 1966; hats and heels, 1959.

I love history, and I love fashion. In fact, the history of societies and cultures is generally told in two ways: through the environments in which people lived and the clothes that they wore. This rich and fascinating history was the basis for my first interest in fashion. Like this wonderful book, I asked myself, "Why'd they wear that?" Fashion is all about context—who, what, when, where—because it is a direct reflection of a time and place. The lavish gowns, wigs, and headdresses worn in the court of Louis XVI of France in the 18th century perfectly captured the extravagant excesses of that time. If you wore that today, people would think that you're going to a costume party. Halloween, anyone?

Clothing is a reflection of a time and a place, but it is also self-expression. The clothes we wear send a message, and those who see us out in the world respond accordingly. Are we covered up and modest? Are we baring a midriff and being daring? Are we fun and flirtatious or serious and commanding? Clothes say those things. Yes, fashion "speaks." For hundreds and in some cases thousands of years, each historical era in every region of the world has a distinct story to tell. Did you know that the ancient Egyptians were a dominant society for 3,000 years and invented tailoring—meaning sharp, crisply constructed clothing? And did you know that the ancient Greeks invented tailoring's counterpart: draping—or cascading, flowing styles? It's all so fascinating. Furthermore, everything you wear today, from jeans and a T-shirt to a shirt and tie to a shift dress, has a history, a distinguished lineage.

Brace yourself for an enthralling journey into the history of fashion! *Why'd they wear that?*

—*Tim Gunn*
OF *PROJECT RUNWAY*

Quick!

Think about your most embarrassing moment ever. Maybe you showed up at a party all dressed up, and discovered that everyone else was casual. Or you came home from school and realized that your fly had been unzipped since lunchtime.

How about your proudest moment? Maybe it was when you were a little kid, wearing your baseball uniform for the first time. Or your new ballet tutu.

What about your craziest dream? Ever dream you showed up at school in your pajamas, or barefooted, or, worst of all, naked?

Clothing plays a role in a lot of major life moments, doesn't it?

Clothing is one of the most fundamental human needs, right up there with food and shelter. We're the only ones in the animal kingdom who change our outer covering on a regular basis. And when we are able to choose what we wear, it becomes fashion.

What people wore can tell us about human history because fashion never stands still. So whether we like it or not, whether we care about fashion or don't give it a second thought, our clothing makes a statement. Fashion really is the mirror of history (as Louis XIV was thought to have said), a visual way to describe a society, and this has been true ever since the moment someone slapped on a fig leaf.

Class Dismissed

Right up until about 80 years ago, a person's clothing announced his or her social status, and everyone knew what the clothes signified. The wealthy dressed one way, the middle classes (if they existed) another, the laboring classes another.

Sometimes middle-class people were able to earn enough money to buy themselves extra clothes, and then the distinctions between classes grew fuzzy. When that happened, rulers tried, often in vain, to enforce "sumptuary laws." These were laws that restricted what people from different ranks of society were permitted to wear. You could be fined for wearing the color purple, or if your ruffled collar was too big, or if the pointy toes of your shoes were too long. There have been periods of history when a person's importance was measured by how much space he or she took up. (Think the puffed-up, broad-shouldered fashions of Henry VIII, the huge skirts of Marie-Antoinette, big hats of bishops, long trains of brides.)

Then, over the course of the 20th century, mass production of clothing leveled the social field. Suddenly it was hard to tell the difference between a lady and her maid, or between the CEO of a company and a junior executive.

Clothes Minded

By studying what people wore, we can learn about how people lived their everyday lives. We can make assumptions about population levels, the way a society felt women should behave, and how much leisure time some people may or may not have enjoyed. We can learn how wide the gaps were between rich and poor. We can even learn something about how parents interacted with their children (or didn't).

Historically, the most outrageous fashions were worn by the wealthy, and to our modern eyes they can look as impractical as they do uncomfortable. Usually the goal of the wearer was to demonstrate to the world that he or she did not have to perform physical labor. Often the fashions were adopted by the middle classes, and almost always, it was the working classes that created them. Working people tanned the leather, wove the cloth, dyed the textiles, and sewed and embroidered the dresses.

Some fashions were also life threatening. Today we ask why people painted their faces with liquid lead, or squashed their internal organs with corsets. But maybe it's just easier for us to recognize these trends after they've happened. If you look around a bit, you'll find some fashions today that may strike future people as equally foolhardy. Why do you see women in our day and age wearing shoes with paper-thin soles and spindly heels—in the dead of winter? Why do people pay to have their faces injected with a known poison in order to smooth wrinkles? And why are some cosmetics manufacturers still adding lead to lipsticks and mercury to face creams?

Now take a minute to consider what you are wearing right now. Have you ever looked at the tags on your clothes to see where they were made? You might be surprised to see how many were made in foreign countries, which would not have been the case 150 years ago.

Everything you're wearing has a history. There's a story in every sneaker, shirt, and stitch.

Wrapping and draping the body was an art form in the ancient world, long before buttons and snaps and zippers existed.

10,000 B.C. - A.D. 1000

THE ANCIENT WORLD
10,000 BC – AD 1000

THAT'S A
WRAP

STEPPIN' Out

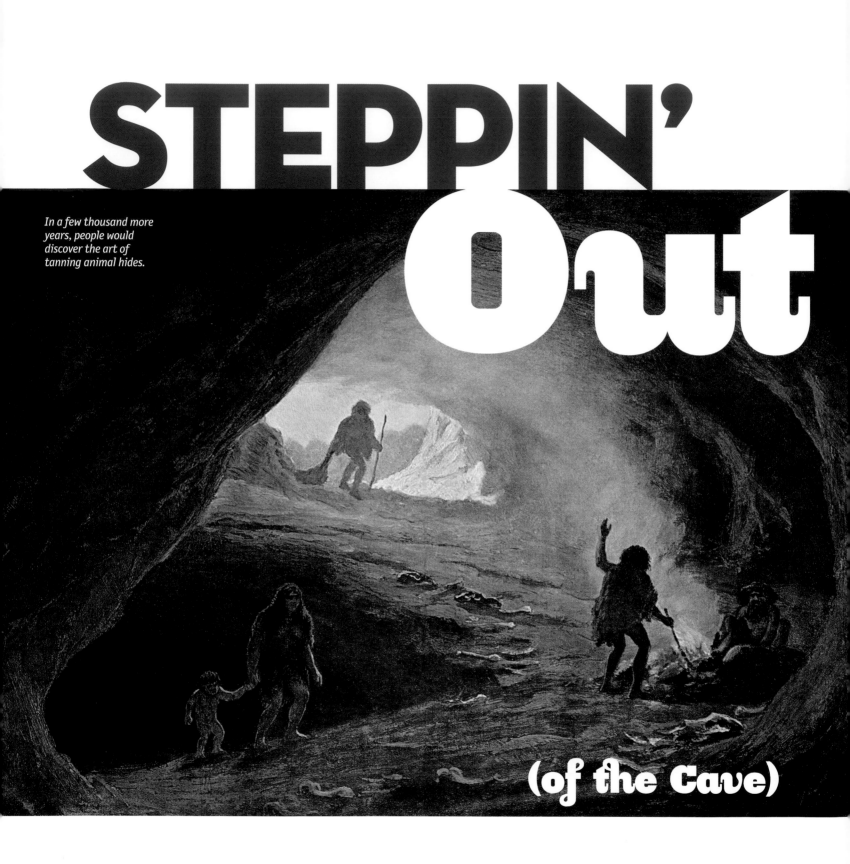

In a few thousand more years, people would discover the art of tanning animal hides.

(of the Cave)

FIRST TEXTILES

Indus Valley Region, 8000 – 2000 B.C.

About 10,000 years ago the Ice Age ended, the sun came out, and people emerged from their caves. Casting off their smelly bearskins to bask in the sunshine, they took up sheepherding and farming and settled down into communities. These first civilizations sprang up in the fertile river valleys in what are now Iraq and Pakistan.

Eventually people began to domesticate sheep to make wool. They grew flax (7000 B.C.) and cotton (5000 B.C.). They learned to spin fibers into thread and weave thread into textiles. Linen (which was made from flax) and hemp (a coarser and scratchier version of linen) became the most common textile materials.

Around 5000 B.C. people also worked out a way to keep animal skins from stiffening up and rotting away. The smelly but highly useful art of tanning leather evolved. Tanning became the preferred method of softening animal hides, as it didn't require chewing them (for more on tanning, see Tough Job: Tanner, page 88).

In the Indus Valley city of Mohenjo Daro (2500–1500 B.C.), people dyed their clothing different colors using various natural dye sources, and both men and women wore jewelry, made from shells, colored stones, and animal teeth.

SEW *What?*

THE FIRST NEEDLES were invented about 10,000 B.C., and were made from woolly mammoth tusks, bird bones, fish bones, or bamboo. Thread was made from animal guts or hair.

At some point during our prehistory someone figured out how to twist together two pieces of fiber to make string. Now they had a material that was not only strong but also allowed shorter fibers to combine to make longer ones. Weaving and textile making became possible.

Bamboo

TOUGH JOB: *Flax Retter*

LINEN IS MADE FROM THE FIBERS of a flowering plant called flax. Making linen is a tedious process—and before machines did much of the work, it was really tedious.

The retter (a word that's closely related to "rotter") harvested the flax plants and set out the stems to rot in the sun. Once the woody outer stalk rotted away, the inner fibers could be separated and spun into linen. This process could take three or four weeks, and required constant watching, to be sure the plants didn't rot unevenly. So the job was a bad combination of boring and hard. A somewhat less time-consuming way to rot and separate the fibers was by soaking the plant stems in water, but this process produced a horrible, putrid smell as the soaking stems rotted. Sometimes retters got around that stinky standing water problem by soaking the plants in running water, but that made retters unpopular with the people who lived downstream.

After the retting was done, the fibers were spun into thread, dyed, woven into linen cloth, and sewn into garments.

Nowadays, the retting process can be done w[ith] [chemi]cals, although in many parts of the world it's still do[ne]

SILK SECRETS

ALL THE RAGE

China, 2600 B.C. – A.D. 1000

The secret of silkmaking was discovered in China more than 4,000 years ago, and for almost 2,000 years, the Chinese kept it a closely guarded secret. With the emergence of the Roman Empire (27 B.C.), the demand for silk grew. The Romans were crazy about silk for its beauty, comfort, and ability to keep one warm in winter and cool in summer. They didn't like the heavy brocade fabrics the Chinese produced, so their weavers simply unraveled the thread and rewove it into sheer, gossamer fabric.

Meanwhile, the Romans kept trying to guess how silk was made. They were positive it came from a plant, the way flax and cotton did. In 70 B.C. Pliny the Elder, a Roman, wrote a 37-volume history of the natural world that became the go-to source on natural history for 1,400 years; in it, he wrongly declared that silk was made from the downy undersides of leaves.

The last thing the Romans would have guessed was how silk was actually produced. Raw silk is made only by the silkworm, not an actual worm but the larval form of the moth *Bombyx mori*. After chomping its way through huge amounts of mulberry leaves (its preferred food and the only thing that causes it to

TOP: *Silkmaking is a time-consuming process. It takes 350 cocoons to make one pair of silk stockings, 630 for a blouse, and 3,000 for a kimono.* RIGHT: *It takes three days for the worm to spin its cocoon, tossing its head in a figure eight motion about 300,000 times.*

produce silk), the caterpillar secretes a gooey substance that hardens into its cocoon. The cocoon can be soaked and unspooled into fine threads.

By about 200 B.C., the secret art of silk made its way to Korea, Japan, and India, and then to Persia. But although people living farther to the west eventually discovered that it was made from moth cocoons, the means to produce it—silkworms and mulberry plants—were not available to them.

Then in A.D. 552 the Byzantine emperor Justinian, responding to growing demand for silk and tired of the exorbitant prices he had to pay for it, sent two monks to China to smuggle out some silkworm eggs. They stashed the eggs in the hollowed-out bamboo staffs they carried. They also managed—somehow—to smuggle out young mulberry shrubs, and to keep them alive and watered

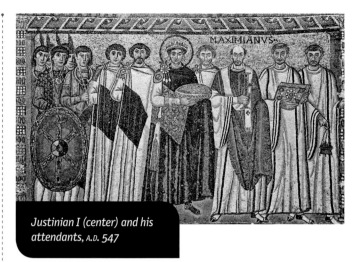

Justinian I (center) and his attendants, A.D. 547

on the long trip home—which may have taken as long as two years. The East Asian and Persian silk monopolies were finally broken, and silk made Byzantium rich and powerful. (The monks received a large monetary reward for their efforts.)

SILK Road

IN 126 B.C., EMPEROR WU TI opened a 6,000-mile (9,650-km) trade route between China and Rome, passing through the hands of Parthians, Persians, and other middlemen who controlled points along the route and who jacked up the prices of the silk. The perilous caravan route went through some of the most inhospitable terrain on Earth. Merchants braved sandstorms, bitter cold, and robberies. The route passed through the dreaded Taklimakan and Gobi deserts, and through mountain passes, where temperatures could range from 122 degrees Fahrenheit (50°C) in summer to minus 50 degrees Fahrenheit (-45.5°C) in winter. The route became known as the Silk Road. It was not an actual road but rather an enormous network of trading pathways. Not just silk came from the East, but also jade, spices, tea, and gunpowder. These were traded for goods from the West, like glass, cotton, wool, gems, ivory, and horses.

Camel caravan on the Silk Road

Caulk
LIKE AN
EGYPTIAN

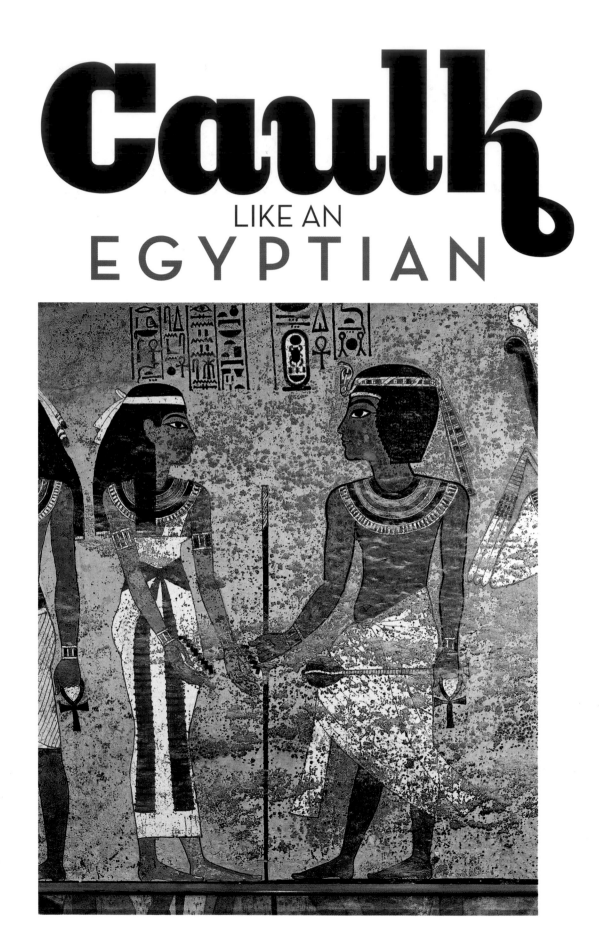

DRESSED TO IMPRESS

Ancient Egypt, 2000 B.C.

Ancient Egyptians prized clean lines. Their art shows men wearing plain loincloths and women straight, simple linen dresses. (Common laborers probably went naked.) They also spent a lot of time grooming themselves.

Both genders wore wigs and makeup. They scrubbed with pumice (a gritty stone) to remove body hair, and slathered lead paste on their faces for an even complexion. Men and women also wore eye paint—kohl for rimming the eyes and darkening the brows and a ground-up green malachite for eye shadow. The malachite came with an added bonus: Its antibacterial properties helped protect the eyes from a biting fly that could cause blindness. And the thick black eyeliner also gave the person added protection from sun glare—much the way a baseball player's eye black does today.

Perhaps because so much skin was exposed to the drying sun, Egyptians used liberal amounts of oil on their bodies, made from animal fat, olive oil, and other plants. Hair could be conditioned with a paste made from gazelle dung and hippopotamus fat. At dinner parties slaves placed cones of perfumed animal fat on guests' heads. Over the course of the evening, the fragrant grease melted and ran down the hair and neck, scenting and conditioning the hair and bathing the wearer in fragrant grease. Scent cones were not just for the wealthy. Musicians, dancers, servants, and children all wore them as well.

Egyptians in all social classes took their oils and unguents seriously. Soldiers and laborers were allotted a certain amount of scented oils as part of their pay.

OPPOSITE: Egyptians preferred linen to wool, and their fashion didn't waver for at least 3,000 years. ABOVE: Ancient Egyptian laborers working on the giant tomb of Ramses III walked off the job when their provisions—including scented ointment for their skin—were delayed. RIGHT: Black galena and green malachite on the lids could protect the eye from sun glare and insects—and it looked good, too. Men were as heavily made up as women.

The joyful depictions of life in ancient Crete show that both men and women wore their hair in long, corkscrew ringlets.

MINOANS

JUST WANNA HAVE *fun*

DRESSED TO IMPRESS

Crete, 2000 B.C.

At just about the same time as the Egyptian civilization, a sophisticated Bronze Age civilization emerged on the island of Crete. Named after their legendary king Minos, the Minoans developed writing, impressive plumbing—and fashions. The Minoans seem to have been a peaceful lot—their castles are unfortified and there are no scenes of war in their artwork. They prospered through trade with their neighbors. They loved colorful clothing and glittery ornamentation. In their artwork they dance, enjoy bountiful feasts, and play lyres, flutes, and trumpets.

Both men and women wore their hair curled and coiled with falling ringlets to the shoulders. The men's skirts—all right, we'll call them tunics—stopped at the knee or a bit below. The women's skirts were remarkable. Brightly colored and bell-shaped, they fell to the ankles, and may have been stiffened with metal hoops that widened as they reached the ground. On top women wore an open jacket with nothing underneath.

A favorite pastime for both men and women was the sport of leaping over bulls for fun, wearing nothing but tightly fitting, body-revealing loincloths.

ABOVE: Don't try this at home.
BELOW RIGHT: Binding the head between two boards began four or five days after a Maya birth and lasted for two or three years. Remarkably the practice usually did not result in permanent brain damage.

Minoan women enjoyed a great deal of freedom—they're pictured sharing meals with men, venturing freely in public, and attending the theater. Most of the Cretan deities are female.

The Minoans also appeared to have prized fit bodies and narrow waists. Both men and women wore wide, tight belts with rolled edges. Some historians have suggested that these metal belts were riveted to the waist in a person's youth and were worn for the rest of their lives—incentive to lay off those honey-soaked dates.

About 1500 B.C. a tidal wave seems to have struck the island, after which inhabitants of the nearby Greek city-state, Mycenae, took control. The Mycenaens were considerably more belligerent and less fun than the Minoan people. (Four hundred years later, the Greek epic poet Homer would write about the Mycenaen siege of Troy in his *Iliad*.)

MAYA & ELONGATED HEADS

FASHION DISASTER

Yucatán Peninsula, 2600 – 900 B.C.

The Maya were a civilization of people who lived on the Yucatán Peninsula in what is now Mexico. Wealthy and powerful Maya adopted the custom of tightly bandaging their babies' foreheads with pads and bindings, or wrapping the forehead between two boards. Having a misshapen cranium was a very visual symbol that your family had a high social status. People did it for religious and social reasons, but also, it seems, because they thought it looked good.

Techniques varied; sometimes the result was a flat, high forehead. Sometimes the skull grew to resemble the shape of an ear of corn. Later the Huns would do the same, for intimidation (see Here Comes the Hun, page 31).

Dressed for battle, with stocking seams straight and not a curl out of place.

Warrior Wear

DRESSED TO KILL

Assyria, 1200 – 600 B.C.

Assyrian warriors sported woolen tunics, pointy helmets, and major attitudes. Their curious headgear helped protect them from "whirlers," opponents who twirled and then flung sharpened stones, often from as far as 650 feet (198 m) away, with deadly accuracy. Assyrian armor was made of overlapping pieces of leather, resembling fish scales.

The Assyrians roared down from the hills and into Mesopotamia—the fertile land between the Tigris and Euphrates Rivers in what is now Iraq—around 1200 B.C. They terrorized most of western Asia for about 600 years.

Assyrian artists left behind a rich visual history. But where their contemporaries, the Egyptians and Minoans, spent their time painting cheerful pictures of parties and feasting, Assyrian artists depicted mostly war images.

To be fair, the Assyrians invented quite a few useful things. They improved the process of tanning leather. They invented locks and keys, magnifying glasses, libraries, postal systems, and the seven-day week. And fashion was important to them. Assyrian warriors rode into battle rouged and perfumed, with curled and coiffed hair and beards. The male warriors even wore a form of fishnet stockings.

21

INDIGO
&
WOAD

THE **COLOR**

COCHINEAL
&
MADDER

PURPLE

SAFFRON
&
WELD

DRESSED TO IMPRESS

Ancient Tyre, 900 – 600 B.C.

Nowadays practically all fabric dye is produced synthetically in a laboratory (see Colorful Clothes and the Color of Money, page 136). But prior to the mid-1800s, clothing colors could be created only with stuff found in nature. Reds came from madder, a plant with red roots (and later, from cochineal insects; see Seeing Red, page 54). Yellows came from weld and from saffron (both flowering plants). Blues came from other flowering plants—woad and indigo (see Tough Job: Woad Maker, page 30, and Indigo Production, page 98). Brown dyes could be made from oak bark, wood, and walnut husks.

But purple was the most rare and costly color of all.

Tyrian purple, as it came to be known, was produced by Phoenician people in the city of Tyre. They were known to the Greeks as *Phoinikes,* or "purple men." Tyrian purple was sought after by Roman emperors and imperial monarchs throughout Asia. And it came from an unlikely source: snail snot.

Tyrian purple was produced from the mucus of the hypobranchial gland of a certain species of mollusk known as *Murex brandaris.*

The Phoenicians lived in a coastal area east of Egypt on a strip of land in what is now Lebanon. Although the Minoans were probably the first to make purple, back in 2500 B.C., it was the Phoenicians who produced enough of the stuff to trade and grow prosperous. The Phoenicians were

Nowadays the color "royal purple" is easy to create, but in ancient times only royalty could afford to wear it.

TOUGH JOB: Dye Producer

MURICIDS ARE A CERTAIN TYPE of sea snail with a gland that secretes a snotlike substance that turns different colors when exposed to sunlight.

The Phoenicians established beachside dye centers wherever they found significant populations of these spiny-shelled creatures. Heaps of ancient shells, discarded by the Phoenicians, can still be found today.

Each *Murex brandaris* produces just two drops of a milky-looking secretion. Dyers had to crush thousands of snails to produce enough dye for just one toga. After being ground up, the dead snails were left in the sun to rot. The oozy slime they secreted was painstakingly collected. By carefully timing its exposure to sunlight, dyers created colors from green to violet to red, to the most prized, an almost-black purple. The smell from the rotting snails was so awful that no one could bear to live nearby.

skilled craftsmen and excellent sailors. They traded their goods all around the Mediterranean. They may have been the first to use the North Star to guide their ships at night.

As demand for the color purple grew, Phoenician traders traveled to places across the European continent and along the north coast of Africa. Their civilization was eventually conquered, first by the Assyrians, and then by the Babylonians.

By then others had learned how to make the purple dye, but producing it didn't get any less labor intensive, and purple remained rare and costly for centuries, worn only by kings and queens. With the expansion of trade following the Crusades (see The Crusades, page 43), and the growing awareness of Eastern cultures during the Renaissance, the demand for exotic dyes from the "Orient" spread across Europe.

Eventually, Tyrian purple was replaced by a new purple dye, made from a species of lichen, that was much less expensive to produce. But the term royal purple remains part of our language to this day.

OLYMPIC ATHLETES

WHAT NOT TO WEAR (CLOTHES)

Greece, 300 B.C.

We think of Greeks as prizing the human figure, perhaps because so many of their statues are naked. But although Greek men walked around naked pretty regularly at the baths and at the gymnasium, women weren't supposed to.

In ancient Greece both men and women wore a chiton, or tunic, of wool or linen, pinned together at the shoulders. Athenians considered it a mark of fine breeding to be able to drape your chiton artfully. Men wore it to the knee, women to the ankle. Women sometimes wore an outer robe, or peplos, belted at the waist.

Greek citizens spent much of their time at the gymnasium (derived from gymnos, *meaning "naked"). It was a place where men could exercise, bathe, and hear a lecture without the bother of wearing any clothes.*

Below: You might think from looking at Greek statues that chitons were always white. In fact, many were dyed bold colors. RIGHT: At first the Greeks, and later the Romans, regarded Scythian trousers as barbarian wear. But trousers were very practical for riding astride a horse.

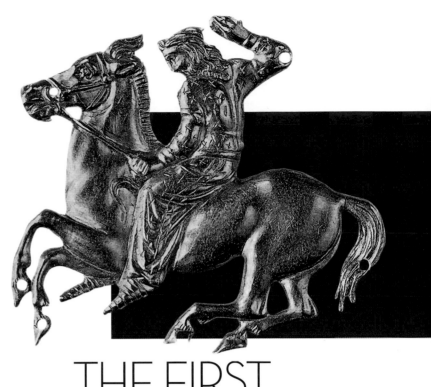

In rival city-state Sparta young girls often left the sides of their chitons unsewn, exposing a good part of the thigh when they walked. And Spartan girls shocked Athenians when they dropped their peplos altogether and entered athletic contests naked, alongside boys. An outraged Athenian writer named Euripides sputtered, "Wish as you might, a Spartan girl never could be virtuous. They gad abroad with young men with naked thighs, and with clothes discarded, they race with 'em, wrestle with 'em. Intolerable!"

At the Olympic Games, the athletes—all male—competed naked. Not only were women forbidden to compete, they couldn't even watch. Any woman caught in the audience could be hurled to her death off a cliff.

One woman supposedly defied the rule. In 338 B.C., the mother of one of the athletes disguised herself as a male trainer to watch her son. When he won his contest, she leapt up to cheer, forgetting her disguise; her cloak slipped off her shoulders, revealing her to be a woman. She was spared death because her son had won a victory wreath.

Sculpture of a Spartan girl in a chiton

THE FIRST PANTS

DRESSED TO FUNCTION

Southern Russia, 331 B.C.

The Scythians were a fierce nomadic tribe that grazed their herds on the steppes, the vast grasslands of central Asia between Manchuria and Russia. Members of this tribe spent a big part of their lives on the backs of their small, fast horses. They were probably the first to use saddles. Skilled riders could turn in the saddle and shoot a bow and arrow at full gallop. We're indebted to the Scythians for a major fashion first—trousers. For a lifestyle spent largely on the back of a horse, trousers worked a great deal better than togas, tunics, or chitons.

The Greeks and the Persians who lived in the vicinity of the Black Sea came into contact with the Scythians. Most Greeks considered trousers indecent, yet many ended up adopting the Scythians' long trousers anyway. The Macedonian warrior Alexander the Great realized their practicality, and he equipped his soldiers with Scythian-style breeches.

25

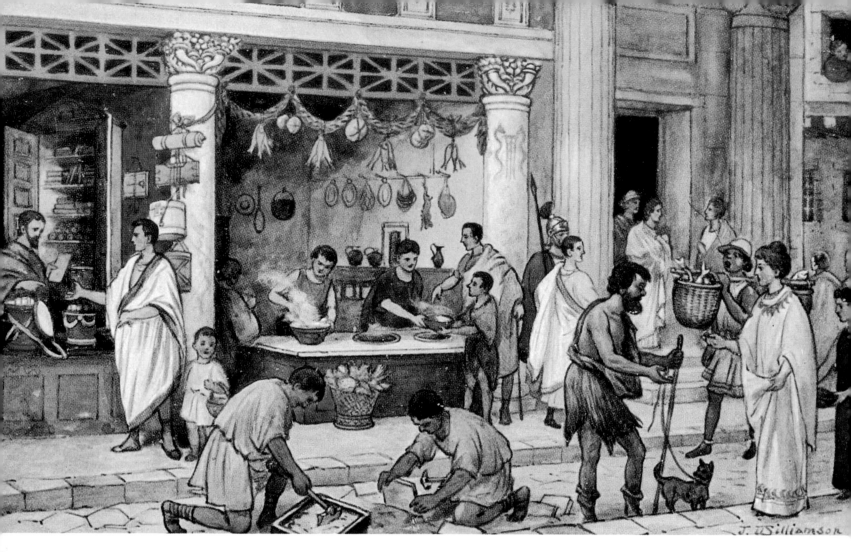

THERE'S NO PLACE LIKE
ROME

DRESSED TO IMPRESS

Ancient Rome, A.D. 27 – 476

Imagine yourself standing in a public square in ancient Rome on a typical market day. You would see teeming crowds of people dressed in a wide array of styles—freeborn Roman men in white togas; well-to-do Roman women, their hair elaborately coiffed and wearing colorful, flowing garments called stolas; laborers, children, and slaves in simple tunics belted at the waist; still other slaves, as well as visitors from the provinces, dressed according to the customs of their homelands, some sporting beards, tattoos, sturdy boots, or leather trousers.

To fully appreciate why Roman inhabitants wore such a wide variety of fashions, you have to understand how deeply stratified (divided) Roman society had become by the height of the empire. Every major conquest by Rome's powerful armies resulted in a new influx of slaves. Tens of thousands of men, women, and children were captured and transported back to Rome. They came from vastly different cultures from faraway frontiers, including Britain, Carthage, Macedonia, Greece, Egypt, Gaul, Nubia, Armenia, and Spain. This varied population mixed with the existing one, swelling the numbers of the city.

Some historians estimate that there were 650,000 slaves in Rome in 100 B.C. That may have been as much as a third of the city's population. One proposal in the Senate was that slaves should be required by law to wear a similar sort of dress so that they could be more readily identified. The proposal was voted down for fear the slaves would realize they outnumbered their captors and revolt.

THAT'S A Wrap

PREDATING THE ROMAN TOGA by at least 3,000 years was the sari, a draped dress made from a single, long piece of fabric worn by Indian women. The loose, wrapped garment was more comfortable than fitted clothing in the hot climate, and before synthetic material was invented, would have been made from lightweight cotton or silk.

Hollywood has popularized the idea of galley slaves chained to their oars, but the ancient Romans probably didn't use slaves for this job.

WELL-TO-DO ROMAN WOMEN SPENT a lot of time on their hair. As the empire progressed, hairstyles grew more and more elaborate. Platoons of slaves were needed to construct and arrange these coifs, and also to aid the Roman woman with the rest of her beauty regimen.

If she was really wealthy, a Roman woman also employed some *cosmetae*. These were slaves whose job it was to remove stray hairs from the body and to help apply makeup. Then there was yet another team of slaves called *parasitae* who stood there and praised the final outcome.

Makeup consisted of red lead or plant dyes to tint lips and cheeks, white chalk or lead to whiten the brow, and ashes or powdered antimony for eye shadow. To achieve a nice pasty consistency, your slave might spit into your cheek powder before slathering it on your face.

Hairstyles were so important to fashionable Roman women that they sometimes paid artists to sculpt their likeness with removable stone wigs.

Prostitutes were required by law to have yellow hair (dyed or wigged). But blond hair became fashionable with many well-to-do Roman women as well. To achieve very vivid shades they used caustic dyes, which could lead to baldness. If one lost one's hair, there were always blond wigs to be imported from Germany or Britain. Those who preferred reddish tints could use henna (a plant-based dye). Black hair could be achieved by mixing leeches with vinegar and allowing the mixture to rot in the sun for two months, after which it could be applied to the hair.

A few Roman men wore wigs, too. Others had fake hair painted onto their bald heads. The ultimate status symbol was to powder your hair with pure gold.

Once dressed and coiffed, it was off to the baths in the afternoon for many wealthy Romans—after which the process would need to begin all over again.

The toga was the garment that separated freeborn male citizens from everyone else. This semicircular piece of white or off-white wool was draped around the body in artful folds and pleats. Under the toga men wore a tunic, a simple garment fastened at the shoulders that reached to the knee and doubled as a sleeping chemise. A vertical stripe of color on the shoulder of the tunic marked your rank in society— scarlet and purple bands were reserved for magistrates and priests.

By law every male citizen was expected to wear a toga for public functions. But many didn't wear theirs. Why did so many men object to wearing a toga? For one thing, it was a clumsy garment. Draping it properly was nearly impossible to do without the assistance of a slave or two. And once you'd been wrapped, you had to keep the folded parts in place without any pins or fasteners, clamping your left arm to your side, as though nursing a constant side-ache. The wearer could gesture with his right hand, but that was about the extent of the physical activity the garment permitted.

Because the toga discouraged physical activity, it became a mark of status to wear one. Like ruffs and corsets of later eras, the toga was meant to show that you were a person who couldn't possibly perform physical labor.

Most men took to wearing their tunics for everyday wear. They wore their togas just for special functions.

BOYS IN BLUE: CELTIC WARRIORS

DRESSED TO KILL

Europe, Western Asia, 500 B.C. – A.D. 500

For a Roman soldier, it must have been rather startling to encounter a Celtic opponent on the battlefield. Celtic warriors were tall—many stood well over six feet (1.8 m)—mostly red-haired, and blue-eyed. They often sported huge, droopy moustaches. And they usually fought naked.

Well, nearly naked. Many decorated their bodies with tattoos and blue paint (called woad), and wore lots of gold jewelry. By the first century B.C., Celtic warriors began to wear chain metal and trousers into battle, and bronze helmets with pointy horns projecting from them, which made the wearer appear even taller (and scarier). Another favorite Celtic accessory? Human heads attached to the belt. Celts believed the human soul was in the head. So they often collected the heads of conquered enemies and took them home.

Celts prized physical fitness and disapproved of middle-aged paunchiness; in Celtic society you could be fined if your belt needed lengthening.

The Celts lived in a vast territory, from northern Scotland to southern Portugal, across a big chunk of Europe, and even into Asia. They probably wouldn't all have referred to themselves as Celts, as there were many different tribes, but their languages were closely related and they shared many of the same customs.

The Romans called them barbarians, but then, Romans tended to call everyone who wasn't Roman a barbarian. Because the Celts kept no written records, it isn't easy to uncover their version of history. But luckily for historians, the Celts had a habit of chucking their valuables into bogs and lakes, or burying valuable items along with their

Celtic warriors were tall—

MANY STOOD WELL OVER SIX FEET (1.8 M)—MOSTLY RED-HAIRED, AND BLUE-EYED. THEY OFTEN SPORTED HUGE, DROOPY MOUSTACHES. AND THEY USUALLY FOUGHT NAKED.

dead. Archaeologists have learned about the Celts from the artifacts found at these sites.

At home, Celtic men wore shaggy fur capes and trousers. Women wore shaggy fur capes and tunics. Women enjoyed a higher status in Celtic families than did women in Rome. Celtic women could own property. Some were even rulers and war leaders. These customs appalled the Romans, who considered women to be their husbands' property.

The Romans learned quite a few things from the Celts. The Celts were skilled metal workers, and they invented chain mail in 300 B.C., which the Romans then copied. The Romans also copied the Gallic Celts' helmet style, which featured cheek guards.

The Celts' love of bling did not escape the notice of the Roman general Julius Caesar, who was looking for cash to pay off his many debts back home. He invaded and conquered Gaul (the region occupied by French Celts) between 58 and 52 B.C. (He went on to become Rome's first emperor, and was assassinated in 44 B.C.—Shakespeare later wrote a play about him.)

In A.D. 43 the Romans finally made their way across the English Channel and invaded Celtic Britain. Gold, silver, and lead mined from occupied Celtic territories enriched the Roman Empire for centuries.

Under Roman occupation, many Celts adopted Roman dress. The men shaved off their big moustaches and gave up wearing furs and trousers, donning togas instead.

But Celtic fashions, in turn, influenced the Romans. Back home, Roman women began wearing more ornamental jewelry, especially gold. Many women also dyed their hair blond in imitation of the blond tresses of many of the women from occupied lands (see Rise & Fall of Roman Hairdos, page 28).

TOUGH JOB: 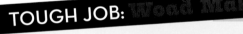 Woad Maker

PRODUCING BLUE DYE FROM WOAD

is a smelly job. Woad is a plant *(Isatis tinctoria)* that used to be found throughout Europe. The leaves were picked, then crushed and kneaded into balls, which turned the workers' hands black. The balls were dried and ground into powder. Then the powder had to be watered and allowed to ferment and oxidize. This process was called couching. When it was dry, the powdered woad was packed up and sent to the dyer.

The dyer poured hot water onto the woad and mixed it with urine. Then the mixture was left to ferment for several more days. The fermentation process produced a horrible, sulfurous odor, which smelled, frankly, like poop. But it did turn fabrics a lovely shade of blue.

Woad has antiseptic properties and may have been used to help heal battle wounds.

Woad was used in England to dye the coats of military officers and policemen as late as the 1930s.

HERE COMES THE HUN

DRESSED TO CONQUER

Central Asia, A.D. 450

Another nomadic tribe, the Huns, galloped onto the steppes (see The First Pants, page 25) about A.D. 430, perhaps from Mongolia. Under the leadership of their fierce chief, Attila, the Huns proceeded to terrorize and conquer most of Europe and Asia. To intimidate their enemies, the Huns bandaged the heads of their own children to flatten their noses and deform their skulls. (See also Maya & Elongated Heads, page 20.) They also appear to have cut away the skin from the cheeks of their male infants, so that they grew up beardless.

Like the Scythians before them, the Huns favored trousers, usually of goatskin. They also wore tunics made from pieced-together rat skins. Or maybe mouse skins. (Most of what we know of the Huns was written by Romans, and we know what the Romans thought about non-Romans.)

Eventually trousers became standard wear among many people in Central Asia. Even women wore them. One fashion historian notes that when a European woman was presented to the Persian court wearing a skirt, "they at first thought she had lost a leg."

VIKI

Toward the end of the eighth century fierce sea warriors from Scandinavian lands terrorized much of northern Europe. These Norsemen, or Vikings, as they came to be known, raced inland along rivers in their beautifully designed longships, the sports cars of their day, sacking villages and plundering riches.

When you think of a Viking, you probably picture a bearded man in a horned helmet. They probably didn't wear those, but they did wear a form of chain mail, and padded leather breastplates.

A suit of mail in the early Middle Ages cost the equivalent of a modern-day sports car.

CHAPTER TWO

THE MIDDLE AGES
1000 – 1400s

KEEPING THE FAITH

Road Trips, Medieval Style · SCRATCHY SHIRTS AND ITCHY BITES · A Rotten, Stinking, Putrid Day at the Office · BOUND AND DETERMINED · Spinning Out · HEAVY METAL · Surely You Joust · BUTTONED UP · Huge Headgear · SCARY SAMURAI · See You in Court

PENITENTS' & PILGRIMS' Robes

During the Middle Ages it was not uncommon to see bands of travelers dressed in white robes, on their way to or from visiting a holy shrine. They had different reasons for deciding to set out on a pilgrimage. Some were landowners, driven out of their gloomy castles by sheer boredom with their lives. These wealthy pilgrims traveled on horseback in relative comfort, spending nights in inns.

Medieval pilgrims arriving at the gates of Jerusalem. Pilgrims collected badges, such as the one pictured top left, and wore them on their hats to show that they had completed the journey.

Other pilgrims were monks or hermits who had dedicated their lives to traveling from one holy shrine to another in order to atone for the sins of men. These sorts might wear wide-brimmed hats decorated with shells and pewter badges collected from all the holy places they'd visited.

But by far the most miserably dressed and bedraggled of this lot were those who'd been assigned to a pilgrimage as a substitute for a prison term—a form of atonement for crimes they had committed.

To understand why these "penitents" were such a common sight in those days, it's important to realize that prison sentences were rare at this time. In fact, outside of a few castle dungeons, hardly any prisons even existed. More often than not, the punishment for most crimes was execution. The method of dispatch depended on the nature of the crime and the social status of the accused.

If a criminal was spared from execution, his punishment tended to match the nature of the crime, although punishments were often much harsher than the crime. Thieves might have their hand cut off, slanderers their tongue torn out, and witches burned to death so as to cleanse the Earth of the witch's evil influence by the "purifying" effect of fire.

But punishment was not the same thing as atonement. Even if you survived your punishment, everyone knew you'd be going to hell unless you atoned for your wickedness by doing penance.

That's where the medieval church stepped in. To atone for their crimes, pilgrims shaved their heads, abandoned their families, and gave up eating meat. They put on long penitential robes (usually white or russet-colored, and patched with crosses), and set out, badly shod or even barefoot, on a very long journey, usually to the distant Holy Land.

TOUGH JOB: Wool Fuller

IF YOU'VE EVER ACCIDENTALLY

thrown a wool sweater into the washing machine and had it come out looking like it might fit your pet Chihuahua, you know that wool is not easy to wash.

Before dry cleaning, before gentle hand-washing laundry soaps, before running water, how did people clean wool?

After the wool was washed, carded, spun into thread, and woven into cloth, fullers soaked the greasy, loosely woven cloth in something alkaline (the opposite of acidic). What was the cheapest and most readily available alkaline cleaner? Urine. It's rich in ammonia, which is an excellent degreaser. The staler and more concentrated the urine was, the better it worked. The fuller tossed the woolen fabric into a vat of urine. Fulling was a very stinky process.

Fullers collected urine from private homes and public toilets. The fuller had to tramp with bare feet on the soaking cloth for hours to get it to the right texture. Then it had to be rinsed and stretched out to dry on hooks, called tenters, where it tightened up and became smooth and soft. Nowadays, with the development of synthetic cleaning products, stale urine is no longer necessary for cleaning wool.

HAIR SHIRTS

Western Europe, 12th century

What's the best way for a pious person to atone for his sins and to mortify his flesh without having to leave home on a long and inconvenient pilgrimage? Wearing a shirt lined with itchy, bristly horsehair. If it becomes riddled with pesky bugs, all the better. One of the most famous wearers of a hair shirt was Thomas Becket (1118–1170).

Becket began wearing a hair shirt soon after he was appointed Archbishop of Canterbury. Perhaps his new clerical position made him feel a sudden urge to mortify his flesh. Perhaps he took to wearing this extremely uncomfortable garment out of remorse for the fun he'd had as the youthful companion to his old friend, King Henry II. Becket's change of attitude from party boy to altar boy dismayed the king, and their friendship strained to the breaking point. Besides wearing the hair shirt, Becket became a vegetarian (during a time when vegetables were reviled by the well-to-do). To top off his extreme virtuousness, every night Becket washed the feet of 13 beggars.

Unfortunately, Becket's newfound piousness made him a lot of enemies among the nobility. In 1170 he was set upon by several armed noblemen and stabbed to death at the altar of the cathedral in Canterbury.

The dead archbishop was found to be wearing layer upon layer of clothing. Working from the outer layers inward, he had on a brown mantle; white surplice; fur coat of lamb's wool; two woolen pelisses; a black, cowled Benedictine robe; a shirt; and underneath it all, a linen chemise lined with itchy horsehair. This tormenting garment was riddled with insects, which came streaming out of it when exposed to the cold air.

Members of the public were outraged by Becket's murder, especially as the king was suspected of having had something to do with it. Stemming from what may have been true remorse, but also to atone publicly for any involvement he may have had in his ex friend's murder, King Henry promised the pope he would perform any penance required. The pope duly ordered the king to set forth on a long and arduous journey to Canterbury on foot—wearing Becket's bug-ridden hair shirt. The weary monarch limped the last three miles (4.8 km) into Canterbury barefooted, with bleeding feet.

KING HENRY II

The murder of Thomas Becket

BOUND FEET

FASHION DISASTER

China, 1200

Throughout history there have been times when people adopted severe and crippling fashions in the pursuit of beauty (see Corsets, page 130, and The Crinoline Craze, page 132). But few practices strike us as more extreme, and incomprehensible, than foot-binding in China. The custom began around the 9th century. By the 13th century it was widely practiced throughout China.

The excruciating, two-year ordeal of foot-binding began when a girl was between the ages of four and seven. The girl's feet were wrapped tightly with linen cloth, her four smaller toes bent under and forced into the sole of her foot, while the front part of the foot was folded under toward the heel. The bandages were tightened regularly until the girl's instep broke and the foot doubled up on itself.

The ideal length of the "Golden Lotus," as the bound foot was called, was three inches (7.6 cm) or less, and the girl was now crippled for life. Often serious complications occurred—the bandages could cut off circulation in the foot, resulting in gangrene and fatal infection. It was not uncommon for a girl to lose one or more toes from the process, and there was always nerve damage. If the girl managed to survive the ordeal, her feet would remain permanently numb, and walking would be intensely painful for the rest of her days.

How could such dangerous and crippling tradition persist for so long? Small feet were thought to be beautiful, and many families believed their daughter had no prospect for marriage if her

Tiny feet—three to four inches (7.6 to 10.2 cm) long—were considered an important status symbol. The x-ray above shows how the binding caused a woman's feet to be deformed.

feet were not bound. Also, deprived of her mobility, the woman became a symbol of her husband's wealth and ability to take care of her.

The practice began among noble women but later spread to all social classes, and it was perceived as a mark of refinement and desirability. It's hard to fathom how working women went about their days so hobbled.

Historians estimate that in the 19th century, 40 to 50 percent of Chinese women had bound feet, and that among wealthy women, the number was close to 100 percent.

Prohibitions against foot-binding were declared as early as the 1700s, and laws were passed after China's revolution of 1911, but it was not until the late 1920s that the government instituted an educational campaign against the practice, along with aggressive enforcement of the law.

WHIRLING DERVISHES

DRESSED TO TWIRL

Balkh (early Afghanistan), 1200s

A dervish is a member of a Muslim religious brotherhood, and the Mevlevi were followers of a certain order of Sufism (a branch of Islam) that originated in the 13th century. The Mevlevi practiced a sacred ceremony in which worshippers—known as whirling dervishes—entered a phase of religious ecstasy by whirling around and chanting to hypnotic music. This dervish order still exists today. The dervishes wear a white gown, a black cloak, and a high brown hat.

Whirling is part of a sacred ceremony. Dervishes who find their spiritual center can spin for hours without throwing up.

EARLY MEDIEVAL
ARMOR

Western Europe, 11th century

Early medieval knights wore shirts made of chain mail. Chain mail had been worn since biblical times, and was made by laboriously connecting metal links, one by one. On their head they sported a hood of mail, which cascaded to their shoulders and left a small opening for their face.

Imagine wearing a metal shirt and shoulder-length metal hood on a hot day in the Negev desert.

41

This mail coat, which was known as a hauberk, weighed about 30 pounds (14 kg). Knights on both sides wore hauberks at the Battle of Hastings in 1066, when the French-speaking Normans invaded Saxon England. By then the cascading chain mail hoods and knee-length coats of mail had become further accessorized with conical metal helmets and attached nose pieces.

Because helmets completely covered the face, it was impossible to recognize anyone. In the confusion and dust and chaos of the battle, knights on each side inadvertently slaughtered some of their own men, unable to distinguish who was on what side.

After that fiasco it became apparent that knights needed labels on the outside of their cans.

The problem was more or less resolved when a French count, Geoffrey IV (1113–1151), noticed while on a Crusade that many of the Muslim soldiers he was battling had distinguishing markings on their outerwear. Accordingly, he stuck a plume of yellow broom (known as *planta genista* in Latin) in his helmet before he rode into battle. His son, Henry II (1133–1189), did the same, and became known as the first of the Plantagenet kings.

Soon most knights adopted crests and other devices to identify which closed-visored knight was which.

Eventually, knights and other noble families designed emblems to express the identity and social status of their family. These first logos were emblazoned on helmets, shields, and surcoats—thus the origin of the term "coat of arms."

European crusaders marching toward battle in the first of what would be a series of bloody conflicts.

THE CRUSADES

Western Europe, Middle East, 1096 – 1272

Today a "crusader" is someone who fights for a cause he or she believes is just and righteous. But the Crusades were a series of holy wars between Christians and Muslims that were fought over the course of several hundred years, beginning in 1096.

Some of the original crusaders may have felt just and righteous about their cause, but others were probably just happy to get away from the grim monotony of their huts or manor houses, and figured a crusade was as good an excuse as any for a little adventure away from home.

By the midpoint of the Crusades, chain mail hoods had been replaced by visored helmets. The knee-length coat of mail evolved into reinforcing plates of metal applied in judicious places around the knight's body, and eventually became full-on body armor. Underneath the helmet and armor, the knight protected himself from painful chafing by first donning heavy quilted padding under the

HOW DID THEY GO TO THE Bathroom?

DIFFERENT STYLES OF ARMOR usually included flaps or ties or trapdoors of one sort or another that allowed the wearer to go to the bathroom—so long as he wasn't in the midst of combat. Battles could last for hours, and no one in his right mind would dismount from his horse to relieve himself when there were enemies around. The knight just "went" inside his armor. It was the job of the knight's squire to clean the armor after the battle, usually with some combination of sand, vinegar, and urine.

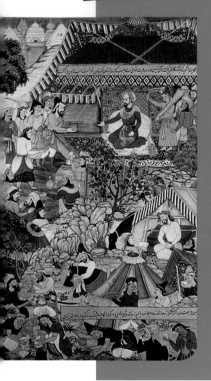

BY 1291 THE MUSLIMS had pushed Europeans out of Jerusalem completely and the Crusades came to an end. While war has few upsides, one of the few positive changes in the West as a result of the Crusades was an increased knowledge of another culture—the Christian crusaders discovered in their Islamic foes a society more civilized, educated, and considerably better washed than their own. Trade routes opened, and suddenly wealthier people's medieval homes became happy recipients of silks, damasks (from Damascus), gauzes (from Gaza), muslins, satins, velvets, tapestries, rugs, dyes, powders, scents, and gems. In the aftermath of the Crusades, huge changes happened in clothing styles, especially for men (see The End of Armor & Chivalry, below).

helmet and a padded tunic under the body armor. This combination of quilting and metal worked reasonably well in protecting the wearer from swords and lances and maces and other accessories wielded by similarly attired foes. But it could also grow unbearably hot inside all that metal and stuffing. Try running around outside on a hot, sunny day in a quilted woolen coat and with a large soup pot on your head, and you'll begin to understand the sort of discomfort faced by crusading warriors in hot desert climates.

To stave off rust in rainy weather, and to keep from roasting inside their metal ovens, knights took to wearing a knee-length surcoat—a sleeveless, ankle-length robe, split up the sides for ease of riding. Yes, adding a coat made it hotter, but it also prevented the sun's rays from glinting off the knight's metal armor, a sure way to announce one's presence to the enemy from far away.

THE END OF
ARMOR & CHIVALRY

DRESSED TO KILL

Europe, 1400 – 1458

The mutual hostility between England and France that had begun in the 11th century at the Battle of Hastings did not improve much over the course of the next 200 years.

The quest for domination over one another's territories culminated in the Hundred Years' War. This new type of war also marked the end of a very uncomfortable fashion—head-to-toe metal suits.

England's King Edward III (1312–1377) was a big, hulking, war-loving jock of a medieval king, a warrior first, and very distantly second, a statesman. In 1337 Edward declared himself the rightful heir to the throne of France, vowing to make it part of England. Thus began the Hundred Years' War.

Skip ahead now to the Battle of Agincourt, October 25, 1415. The English, led by Edward's great-grandson, Henry V (1387–1422), revived Edward III's claim to the French throne and staged an attack on Normandy. Henry's men marched wearily toward a narrow field in Agincourt, where the French army awaited them in far greater numbers (although modern historians have cast doubt on just how heavily outnumbered the English actually were). The French cavalry (knights on horseback) wore plate armor with visored helmets. Armed with lances, shields, swords, and daggers, the two sides marched into battle.

But the French hadn't reckoned on the superiority of the scantily clad English and Welsh archers, who were capable of firing 15 arrows a minute from their deadly longbows. The archers wore jackets and loose tights, called hose. Some were even barefoot from their long march. Many of the archers stripped off their upper garments to make it easier to shoot their bows—the ultimate shirts versus skins contest.

The battle took place in a muddy field between two sets of woods. As the heavily armored French nobles advanced on horseback, they became bogged down in the thick mud, and were massacred by the English longbowmen and by common soldiers wearing much lighter clothing and gear. After numerous volleys of arrows, many of the French knights fell from their horses and simply drowned in the sucking mud, smothered inside their own armor, as other men and horses stumbled over them, while the nimble English archers closed in and hacked the fallen French knights to death through the chinks in their armor.

Shakespeare immortalized the English victory in his play, *Henry V*, but ultimately the English occupation did not last, and the war persisted for several more decades. Still, Agincourt was a military turning point—it marked the end of medieval

Although significantly outnumbered, the common soldiers under England's Henry V outmaneuvered the French nobles in their heavy steel armor.

BUT THE FRENCH HADN'T RECKONED ON THE SUPERIORITY OF THE ENGLISH AND WELSH ARCHERS WHO WERE CAPABLE OF firing 15 arrows a minute ...

After suffering a deadly volley of long-range arrows from the English archers, the heavily armored French knights who fell from their panicked horses found they could not get up. Many simply drowned in the sucking mud.

MODERN-DAY ARMOR

ARMOR HAS MADE A COMEBACK. Modern flak jackets contain a body armor called Kevlar, developed in 1965, which is a lightweight, synthetic material that is five times stronger than steel. It's also used in bulletproof vests. Other body armors have been developed and improved upon, some of which are so tough they can protect a soldier from powerful, direct explosions.

GIRL *Soldier*

JOAN OF ARC WAS A 14-YEAR-OLD illiterate French girl who claimed she heard God speaking to her. She cut off her long hair and dressed as a knight, then led the French armies to victory against the English. Partly because girls weren't supposed to dress like boys (and partly because of politics), the French turned her over to the English after the war, and she was burned at the stake for witchcraft in 1431.

warfare. Kings suddenly realized that peasants could fight against nobles that were on horses, and win. Now kings no longer needed to hire expensive knights to protect the realm. They could use the much more numerous—and expendable—peasants as foot soldiers.

Add to that the fact that knighthood had proved to be too expensive for knights, as well. In order to pay for a suit of armor and a good horse (the equivalent of a high-end sports car in today's dollars), the knight had to sell or mortgage most of his property. He might also have collected money from his peasants who wanted to get out of future feudal duties, thereby freeing them from their bonds. Returning crusaders couldn't pay their bills.

And when armor-piercing firearms became more widely available (in the 15th century), armor became completely obsolete. The medieval social order was changing. Knighthood was going out of business.

It took immense strength to draw an arrow back from the six-foot (1.8-m) longbow—the weight pulled is estimated at 150 to 200 pounds (68–91 kg). The English archers were the elite athletes of their day.

Forward FASHIONS & Funky FOOTWEAR

Europe, 1300s

Fashion in the West hit its stride in the early 1300s. Before then, even wealthy men and women had worn similar garments—straightforward, practical robes (called cotes, and later, more snug-fitting cotehardies) that they fastened at the shoulders, with or without a belt. Peasants wore a version of that, at least in cold weather, although their tunics were shorter to allow them to move around more freely. (In summer many laborers in Europe wore next to nothing.)

Around 1330 things started to change. The invention of the button helped—now your cotehardie didn't have to be lowered over your head, but could be fastened in front or back and could therefore fit the body more snugly (see Buttoned Up, below).

Crusaders returning from the Holy Lands flaunted a new shoe style for men that featured curled-back, pointy toes, stiffened with whalebone. As the fashion evolved, the toes grew and grew until by around 1350 some men sported points two feet (0.6 m) long that had to be tied to their garters. These points made it hard to walk without tripping (if you've ever tried to walk while wearing swimming flippers, you'll have a rough idea). Although armor was on the wane, it still existed for jousting tournaments, and many knights wore metal versions of the pointy-toe fashion.

BUTTONED Up

BEFORE 1330, if you wanted a snug-fitting bodice and sleeves, you had to be sewn into your clothing every day by your servant. But around 1330, the button came into popular use. If you had servants to dress you, your garment buttoned up the back. If you dressed yourself, it buttoned up the front.

BROGUES

IN MEDIEVAL SCOTLAND AND IRELAND laborers wore a special shoe called a brogue. Men punched small holes in the tops of their shoes, which allowed water to drain out when walking through swampy fields. Brogues are worn today as part of business attire, and the perforations are decorative.

POST-PLAGUE FASHION

DRESSED TO THRILL

Europe, late 1300s

SOME OF THE MORE ELABORATE
bridal gowns today include a long train and complicated headgear. Kate Middleton's bridal gown had a 10-foot (3-m) train. Princess Diana wore a 24-foot (7.3-m) veil and a gown with a 25-foot (7.6-m) train.

The Black Death (bubonic plague) had long been known and feared, but in 1348 it wiped out as much as a third of the population of Europe, the Middle East, and North Africa. After that, fashion in many European courts took a curious turn. Pre-plague fashions for both men and women had consisted of long, flowing robes (cotehardies). The only real distinctions between the clothing of the rich and the poor were the colors (bright colors were expensive) and the quality of the cloth. In the aftermath of the plague, long tunics on men grew shorter and shorter until some men's close-fitting coats became scandalously short—sometimes a mere two inches (5 cm) below the belt.

The long, shapeless tunics women had worn in the 13th century now became more fitted to the body. It was indecent for a woman to reveal her arms or her legs, but the bust and the shoulders were another story. Necklines plunged lower and lower, and the waistline became a big focus. During the late 14th century it was raised up over a padded belly in a distinctly pregnant look. Were these fashions an advertisement to the opposite gender of one's availability as a potential mate?

In the 15th century the padded belly fashion continued in the form of high-waisted gowns—for men and women—called houppelandes. The high-end version for women often included elaborate headgear (see Coneheads, opposite), sleeves long enough to trip over, and a long train of extra fabric that trailed behind the wearer. Sometimes page boys walked behind, in order to lift the ends of the train out of the muck—but not always. One could try to gather up the trailing fabric and clutch it to one's middle, but one also had those trailing sleeves to contend with. Given the state of rutted, muddy, dung-filled roads and pathways at the time, servants must have had quite a time keeping the hemlines in any sort of reasonable condition.

To balance the heavy fabric and the weight of your headgear, it was necessary to thrust the hips and belly forward as you walked. This posture shocked the clergy.

You try it! Gather up the comforter from your bed and hold it close to your chest with one hand, while trying to balance a basket of laundry on your head. And then try walking.

CONEHEADS

DRESSED TO THRILL

Europe, late 1300s

During the late Middle Ages, most unmarried girls wore their hair loose and long. Starting around 1360 or so, European women sported some crazy headgear. In France women wore bourrelets—wide, padded rolls on top of the hair—and hennins, towering cone-shaped headdresses, sometimes with draped veils.

The "ram's horn" headdresses were made of wire mesh draped with fabric and could be as long as three feet (0.9 m). By the early 15th century, you might also see a four-foot (1.2-m)-long steeple headdress, a butterfly-shaped gizmo, and a miter shape (like a bishop's hat). Flemish women wore a blunter version of the hennin; Italians wore turban-type designs. Women also plucked their eyebrows and shaved their hairlines to achieve a high forehead underneath this hilarious headgear. Men wore versions of wild headgear as well.

Architects all over Europe had to redesign doorways so women wouldn't bash into them.

Extravagant headdresses like these were often constructed with wire mesh and springy whalebone.

BONFIRE
OF THE
Vanities

Europe, 1400s

No sooner had sumptuous and flamboyant clothing become more widely available than it became a target of church reformers. These reformers preached that it was an act of piety and devotion to God to renounce your wealth, social position, and worldly goods (that is, give away all your stuff). Fancy clothes were a sign of pernicious pride. Some people became so fearful of eternal damnation that they not only threw away their expensive stuff, but they also walked around in hair shirts with pebbles in their shoes (see Hair Shirts, page 38).

SAVONAROLA

Popular preachers such as the Franciscan friar Bernardino of Siena (1380–1444) and the Dominican priest Girolamo Savonarola (1452–1498) staged "bonfires of the vanities," huge fires in outdoor squares where people were encouraged to cast their wigs, fancy clothing, jewels, and other frivolous items into the flames. Unfortunately included among these frivolous items were masterpieces by the artist Sandro Botticelli.

50

SAMURAI **WARRIORS**

Japan, 1300 – 1573

Imagine coming face-to-face in a dark alley with this samurai warrior (right). He would be dressed head-to-toe in armor, from a horned steel helmet on his head down to lacquered leg protectors. On his face he would be wearing a fiercely grimacing mask, intended to intimidate, and on his body, superbly wrought leather (or lacquered iron) body armor. The helmet, or *kabuto*, was especially impressive, with projecting horns or antlers, making the warrior look like a large, angry beetle.

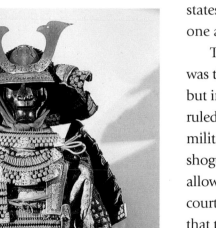

If the look was meant to intimidate people, it certainly worked. (The word "samurai" means "to be on one's guard.") Added to the intimidation factor was the fact that the samurai had permission from his superior officer to cut down any member of the lower classes who might have offended him. He was also allowed to test out the blade of his sword by lopping off the head of anyone of lower rank who happened to be passing by. No wonder these warriors were universally feared.

The samurai class of warriors rose in importance during the eighth century and ended its dominance in 1868 at the end of the Edo period. But their heyday was during the chaotic Muromachi period (1333–1573), when Japanese society was dominated by warring factions and dozens of independent states vying for power over one another.

Theoretically, the emperor was the head of the nation, but in actuality Japan was ruled by the most powerful military officer, known as the shogun. The shogun generally allowed the emperor and his court to maintain the illusion that the emperor was in power. But in fact the shogun was much more powerful. Under the strict class system, the samurai served under local warlords and adhered to a stern code of honor known as Bushido ("the way of the knight"). According to this code, it was the samurai's duty to remain loyal to his superiors, live a hard and frugal life, and to die by his own hand rather than suffer the humiliation of capture or defeat on the battlefield. Every warrior carried a sharp dagger in order to perform, if necessary, a form of ritual suicide known as seppuku (or hara-kiri, as it has come to be more commonly known).

COURT Dress

IN JAPAN court ladies wore multiple kimonos known as *junihitoe*, formal court costume that means "12 layers." Some women wore as many as 20 layers.

The craze among Europeans to explore the globe was prompted by monarchs eager to conquer new territories and by explorers seeking fame and fortune.

10,000 B.C. – A.D. **1000**

1000 – 1400s
THE MIDDLE AGES

1400s – EARLY 1500s
THE AGE OF EXPLORATION

CHAPTER THREE

THE AGE OF EXPLORATION
1400s – early 1500s

GOING GLOBAL

Make New Friends, but Keep the Gold · SCARLET IS THE NEW BLACK · **Nice Work if You Can Survive It** · SOLE SEARCHING · **Footloose and Wrinkle-Free** · A POISONOUS, SUFFOCATING, PERILOUS DAY AT THE OFFICE · **Finding That Fountain** · FROZEN SMILES · **Oh, Smack!**

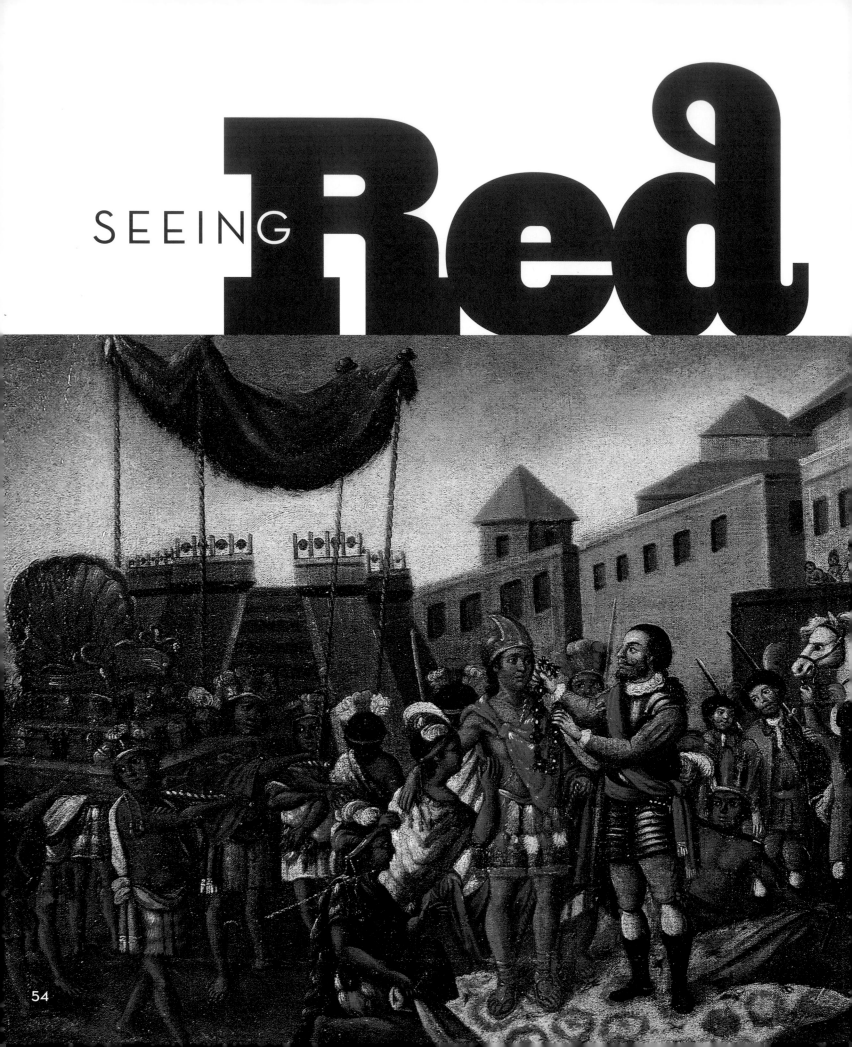

SEEING Red

CHRISTOPHER COLUMBUS

DRESSED TO IMPRESS

Mexico, 1519

In 1492 Christopher Columbus planted the Spanish flag on an island in the Bahamas and declared to the world that he had just arrived in India. He called the natives Indians, which is why the Caribbean Islands have been known ever since as the West Indies. Columbus returned to the New World three times, and he continued to insist that it was India, despite mounting evidence—and increasing suspicion among other explorers—that this land was not Asia at all.

About 20 years later, in 1519, Spanish conquistador Hernán Cortés landed on the shore of what is now Mexico. He was determined to conquer the Aztec people who lived there, claim the land for Spain, and steal all the gold before anyone else could get there first. After a quick look around, Cortés's hopes of finding gold in this new land faded. The dispirited Cortés and his fellow conquistadores began to lose hope of gaining fame and riches. But their hopes rose again when they beheld what the Aztec leader, Moctezuma, and his men were wearing. It was an amazing sight: The Aztec wore red robes of a color more brilliant than anything the Spaniards had ever seen.

It's important for those of us living in this day and age to understand what effect these red robes must have had on Cortés and his men. Many of the conquistadores came from poor backgrounds. In those days, bright colored clothes were a luxury available only to the very wealthy, and brilliant red was one of the two most costly colors (along with purple). How, the Spaniards must have wondered, had these "primitive" natives produced such dazzling hues?

The Aztec were a warrior society that controlled what is now Mexico for most of the 15th and early 16th centuries. While Moctezuma is notorious for the mass human sacrifice rituals conducted under his reign, he ruled over one of the largest, cleanest cities in the world at the time.

But Moctezuma made the fatal mistake of welcoming the Spanish newcomers and peacefully turning control of his kingdom over to them. (According to an Aztec prophesy, a god-king was to appear in the year

WHAT Now?

SMACK! With the invention of synthetic colors in the 19th century, cochineal production declined, but nowadays cochineal red is still used to tint cosmetics like lipstick and blush.

A somewhat stylized interpretation of Cortés meeting Moctezuma. The European painter used a lot of expensive cochineal red paint to render the clothing of both groups, although it's unlikely the conquistadores would have been wearing such vivid reds.

CONQUISTADOR

CONQUISTADOR is the Spanish and Portuguese word for "conqueror," and a term widely used for all the explorers, adventurers, and privateers who conquered, plundered, and brought native people in the New World under the control of Spain and Portugal following Columbus's "discovery" of the New World in 1492.

1519, arriving from the east and bringing glory to the Aztec people. By sheer coincidence and dumb luck, Cortés happened to show up that very year; Moctezuma concluded that he must be that god.) A year later, Moctezuma was killed—it remains unclear whether by the Spanish conquerors or by one of his own disgruntled subjects.

Cortés and his conquistadores, still intrigued by the red robes, swiftly plundered the Aztec kingdom, burned the capital city of Tenochtitlan (now Mexico City) to the ground, and slaughtered most of the inhabitants who hadn't already died of disease. Then, in the midst of their plundering, they discovered several bags containing a mysterious granulated powder. They shipped the powder back to Spain. Although a little slow to realize its value, the Spanish began selling this powder to dyemakers, who realized the potential the brilliant red tint held for textile producers.

The Spanish did not have the expertise to dye textiles themselves, but demand for their red dye grew, and by the late 1560s, Spain was becoming rich. The brilliant red color—called cochineal red—was derived from ground-up insects—*Dactylopius coccus*. (Although even the Spaniards didn't realize the cochineal was actually an insect until as late as 1725. Legless and wingless, the red-producing female insect looks like fluff or mold. If you squeeze one, red stuff comes out. People thought it was a grain, a berry, a seed, a round worm, or even a combination plant-animal sort of "wormberry.")

Cochineal red was much brighter than the reds that dyers were currently using, including kermes (made from any of three other species of insect), or madder, a plant-based source.

Around 1607 an alchemist accidentally discovered that adding acid to the ground-up cochineal solution produced an even more brilliant scarlet. From that point on, the color scarlet became associated with wealth and power, such as Roman Catholic cardinals' scarlet robes, and the red coats of British military officers.

TOUGH JOB: Dyer

THE JOB OF RENAISSANCE DYER was difficult, dangerous, and highly specialized. As one historian notes, the job involved working with "fiery furnaces, boiling water, corrosive acids, poisonous salts, and fuming vats." Although skilled dyers could make a good living producing beautiful fabrics, they did not enjoy a high social status. The dyeing process was extremely smelly, and dyers often dumped their stinking vats of dye solutions into nearby streams and rivers, which made them unpopular with their neighbors. (See also Tough Job: Flax Retter, page 13.)

DRESSED TO FUNCTION

Americas, 1500s

European explorers made other funky fashion "discoveries" that were long known to the native people they conquered. For instance, people of the Amazon rain forest wore rubber shoes made from the milky sap of a special tropical tree. They dipped their bare feet in the sap, and then dried them by the fire. When the sap hardened, it formed a rubbery protective "sneaker," perfect for treks into the dense forest.

North American Indians wore moccasins. Moccasins were made from a single piece of leather gathered around the foot, sometimes it had a reinforced sole. Many Europeans began wearing moccasins as well.

TOP: A Mohican chief sporting moccasins
BOTTOM: Cheyenne moccasins

THE
fountain
OF YOUTH
ALL THE RAGE

Florida, early 1500s

You may have learned about another Spanish explorer, Juan Ponce de León (1460–1521), who famously led an expedition in search of the Fountain of Youth. According to the legend, widely known among Europeans, whoever bathed in or drank from the fountain would never grow old. It's unlikely that Ponce de León would be foolhardy enough to organize an expensive and dangerous expedition into unknown territories just for the purpose of finding this mythical fountain. He was more interested in acquiring gold, glory, slaves, and plunder.

In April 1513 his expedition arrived at what he believed to be an island, and he named it La Florida because it was Easter (in Spanish, *Pascua Florida*) and because the land was lush with flowers and vegetation. (In Spanish, *florida* means "flowery.")

In 1521 he returned to Florida. He was struck in the thigh by an arrow in a fight with the local Indians, and died later of his wound.

How did the Fountain of Youth rumor get started? A few years after Ponce de León's death, an enemy of his chronicled the Spanish settling of the Americas. According to this unflattering account, Ponce de León was deceived by local Indians into believing in the existence of the miraculous fountain. The writer's intent was to show that the explorer was gullible and dim-witted. But the fable has persisted for centuries.

A bemused-looking Indian looks on as Ponce de León tests a fountain for magical qualities. This probably never happened.

BOTOX. Got wrinkles? Nowadays doctors can temporarily smooth out those pesky lines in your face by giving you a shot in your forehead. Inside the syringe is a purified form of one of the most lethal poisons known. (The bacteria *Clostridium botulinum* is found in untreated water and soil, and enters the body through wounds or improperly canned food; it's also found naturally in honey, which is why you should never give honey to an infant younger than one year old.) Botox temporarily "paralyzes" the muscles of the face.

YOUTHFUL FACE CREAMS.

If you think it's funny or crazy that so many people believed the Fountain of Youth existed, consider this: In 2009 Americans spent nearly a billion dollars on creams that claim to "reduce the appearance of wrinkles." Despite the

fact that no permanent cure for wrinkles has yet been discovered, people are still searching for some version of the Fountain of Youth, something that will stave off the aging process. We pay lots of money for face-lifts, dermabrasion (sanding of the skin), microdermabrasion (heavy sanding of the skin), and chemical peels, which basically burn off the top layer of your skin and leave your face as smooth and shiny as a peeled grape. You can also have your facial wrinkles plumped up by having a doctor inject you—in the face—with fat tissue.

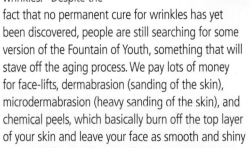

Detail of Peter Paul Rubens's splendid portrait of an Italian noblewoman, 1606. She wears an enormous, gravity-defying cartwheel ruff.

10,000 B.C. – A.D. 1000
THE ANCIENT WORLD

1000 – 1400s
THE MIDDLE AGES

1400s – EARLY 1500s
THE AGE OF EXPLORATION

1500s – EARLY 1600s
THE RENAISSANCE

THE RENAISSANCE
1500s – early 1600s

RUFF & READY

CLOSING THE GAP:
CODPIECES

Europe, late 1400s – late 1500s

By the early Renaissance men's tunics had shrunk to such short lengths that they left a scandalous opening at the place where the tights came together, both in front and back. Tights (called hose) were two separate stockings in those days. So to preserve a man's modesty, a triangular flap—known as a codpiece in England, and a *braguette* in France—closed the gap. The codpiece could be untied so the wearer could go to the bathroom.

During the reign of the English king Henry VIII (1509–1547), men's clothes grew to exaggerated proportions, with wide shoulders, padded sleeves, and boxy torsos. Portraits from that time make men appear as though someone had pumped them up with a bicycle

A highly upholstered, padded king, complete with codpiece

pump. Codpieces enlarged along with every other accessory, to a rather outrageous degree. They were heavily padded into various shapes ranging from a banana to an avocado, and sewn to the front of the breeches at the lower end and then tied at the top, so that the wearer could easily untie it to go to the bathroom. Some men used them as a man-purse, storing snuff, or snacks, or spare change inside them. And because both men's and women's outfits were held together with multiple pins (see The Ruff Collar, page 65, and Frilly & Foppish, page 67) some may even have used their codpieces as—wince—pin cushions.

Codpieces went out of fashion when balloony trunk hose came into fashion (around the 1570s).

GOTH
GOLLY GEE

DRESSED TO IMPRESS

410, 1300, 1800s, and today

The Visigoths were a Germanic tribe that attacked and helped destroy ancient Rome in the fifth century A.D. The men favored belted tunics, bronze horned helmets, and trousers, and the women belted, sleeveless dresses and capes.

The term "Gothic" reemerged about a thousand years later. Gothic refers to a style of architecture in Western Europe from the 12th to the 15th centuries, characterized by pointed arches and flying buttresses, as well as the painting and sculpture from that period. The elongated silhouettes of Gothic cathedrals were mirrored in fashions (see Coneheads, page 49).

In the 19th century a genre of literature emerged that has come to be described as gothic. Gothic stories usually include a gloomy setting, violent events, and a grim tone. (Think *Dracula*, *Dr. Jekyll and Mr. Hyde*, and anything by Edgar Allen Poe.)

In the 1990s a unique style of fashion emerged that was dubbed Goth, and the style has persisted to the present day. People described as Goth have a tendency to look on the dark side, listen to alternative rock, and dress in dark, vampirish clothing. Accessories include spiky hair, heavy black eyeliner, bloodred lipstick, and lots of safety pins.

Three stages of Goths—top left, the Visigoth "barbarians" sacking Rome A.D. 410; center, Milan cathedral, showing the verticality of Gothic-style architecture; top right, some modern-day Goth-style dress

SCRATCH THAT!
FLEA FURS

DRESSED TO IMPRESS

Europe, mid-1500s

Pestered by fleas? You could try a flea fur to rid yourself of those pesky bugs. This solution was popular among Europeans of high rank in the mid-1500s. Here's what you do: Take a small dead animal—head, claws, tail, and all—and drape it jauntily over one of your arms. Then wait for awhile.

The strategy behind flea furs, as they were called, was that the fleas dining off you would decide that it was more fun to dine off the dead animal around your arm instead. After the fleas had leapt onto your flea fur, you could give it a periodic shake and dislodge the bugs. (Flea furs didn't work. People didn't realize that fleas are attracted to warm, living bodies.)

Flea furs were usually small, dead animals such as sable or marten, and the stuffed creatures could be elaborately ornamented. Precious jewels often replaced eyes and claws. Flea furs were an extravagant and costly fad, which originated in Italy and quickly spread to other European courts. Henry VIII owned two flea furs, both of sable. Elizabeth I, his daughter, was presented with at least one as a royal gift.

The fad didn't last very long, although lapdogs may have been an improvement as flea attractors.

In the late 19th and early 20th centuries the fashion for wearing a whole, stuffed animal (called a stole) or many small animals sewn together to make a larger wrap, made a comeback (see Plume Fad, page 154).

Portrait of a woman, 1536, sporting the latest hot accessory

THE Ruff COLLAR

Europe, 1530 – 1630

Ruff collars became all the rage among wealthy courtiers in Europe during the middle part of the 16th century, but eventually everyone wore them, including working people. Even the earliest American colonists, those stern and somber Separatists, brought them along on their journey to the North American wilderness.

The extremely awkward and accordion-shaped collar was made of any length of cloth—from 1.5 yards (1.4 m) for a working person's to many yards long for a deluxe version. Wealthy people's ruffs were made of fine cloth—lawn or cambric.

Early versions began in the Renaissance as a small, gathered-drawstring collar, but quickly grew to an elaborate size. Imagine having a beard and wearing one of these.

A mother and her six children, 1605, all in ruffs. Two of these are boys (see Children's Wear, page 115).

Making a ruff required huge skill and patience. The linen was pleated into folds in a "figure eight" pattern, using a "poking stick," and creased with heated irons. By the 1560s someone figured out how to make starch as a stiffener. Wheat was boiled to a goopy paste, spackled on, and brushed into every fold. The ruff was then dried in front of a fire, before the whole process was repeated. Then it had to be pinned onto a wire support (appropriately named an underpropper), which was in turn pinned to the neckline of the dress or other garment.

Besides making the person look as though his disembodied head were sitting on a platter, ruffs were fragile, expensive, and cumbersome. They drooped in wet weather. They seriously impaired movement. Members of the nobility wore huge ruffs to advertise their leisure status. The wearer was incapable of performing any physical labor, including eating, evidently—any sort of drippy food posed a great hazard to the cleanliness of one's ruff. Spoons had to be made with longer handles to reach the person's mouth. If it did get stained or torn or rained on, it could be sent out to the ruffmaker to be reset: It was laundered, re-pleated, stiffened, and starched. You could also have it set in different-size curves, depending on the current fashion. It's a wonder women didn't trip on a regular basis, wearing a floor-length dress and a ruff so large they couldn't see their feet.

Working people's ruffs were made of coarser material and were usually smaller—maybe just a little frill around the ears—but they must still have seriously hampered a person's movements.

The 16th-century Spanish court favored white ruffs and dark clothes. The somber color tones seemed to complement their severe outlook on life and provided them with a go-to outfit for attending an *auto-da-fé* (Portuguese for "act of faith"), which was a frequently held ceremony during which many prisoners were condemned to death by the church for perceived crimes against God (see Inquisition Wear, below). But when the fashion appeared in the court of Queen Elizabeth I, court ladies wore ruffs in all colors. Favorite ruff colors were white, pale blue, and a special bright yellow extracted from saffron.

INQUISITION Wear

THE SPANISH INQUISITION began in the 15th century and lasted for several hundred years. The mission of the Inquisition was to defend the purity of the (Catholic) faith. Spies of the Inquisition accused people of blasphemous acts. Some of these "crimes" included taking a bath or refusing to drink alcohol. Those accused of crimes against the church often suffered punishments ranging from being forced to wear a *sanbenito* (a penitential robe with a red cross on the front) to long imprisonments, to unspeakable tortures and death. Those who fared the worst were usually people who had converted from Islam or Judaism and were accused of secretly practicing their old faiths.

Prisoners of the Spanish Inquisition wore the sanbenito and also a *coroza*, which resembled a dunce cap. They marched grimly through crowds gathered to witness an auto-da-fé.

This portrait of Elizabeth I was painted in the late 1580s, just after England had beaten back the Spanish Armada and established that it was the reigning power of the day. It symbolizes England's power and dominance.

frilly & foppish

ELIZABETHAN FASHIONS

DRESSED TO IMPRESS

England, late 1500s – early 1600s

Queen Elizabeth I (1533–1603) loved clothes, and she knew that fabulous fashion impressed people. She may have owned as many as 3,000 gowns. The queen expected people in her court to dress well, too. For men as well as women, an outfit could cost as much as a house.

QUEEN ELIZABETH OF BOHEMIA
The tilted farthingale allowed the wearer a place to rest her hands on the ledge of the skirt.

During Elizabeth's reign, female court dress became so stiff and stylized it makes your neck ache just to look at it. Nearly every part of the outfit was artificially molded in some way or another—the V-shaped bodice; whalebone-stiffened waist (not yet called a corset, but basically a corset in principle); wired, puffed out sleeves; and most dramatically, the wide skirt called a farthingale (see Hoop Skirts, page 108).

Have you ever watched a young child draw a picture of a princess? She probably draws a lady in a long gown that puffs out at the sides. Such skirt-shaping devices really did exist. A version of the poufy gown has made three distinct appearances over the past 400 years. The skirt-shaping trends originated with royalty, but the fashion usually became popular in every class, and even working women managed to contrive some way to mimic the look.

The first version of poufy skirts was the farthingale. It appeared in Spain in the early 1500s, but the fashion soon spread to other European courts, and then to all classes of women. The farthingale (or *vertugado,* or *verdingale)* was a petticoat reinforced by a series of hoops made of wire or whalebone or bent willow branches.

Around 1570 a variation appeared, known as a wheel farthingale, which Queen Elizabeth adopted. This version involved tying a padded roll around the hips, over which the skirt was draped. The rolled underskirt caused one's dress to stick out at right angles from the waist, sometimes as far as four feet (1.2 m) from side to side. The skirt was pinned at the top and fell in pleats, in a shape roughly like a soda can. The skirt was held in place by hundreds of pins to get the pleating to look just so.

The bewildering vocabulary of clothing items for Elizabethan women includes busks, bodices, scarves, puffs, ruffs, cuffs, muffs, partlets, frislets, and bandlets. It could take a woman (and her maid) hours to arrange her hair, pin and tie the garments onto her body, apply cosmetics, starch and pin her vast ruff, sew jewels and sleeves onto her gown, and pin the flounce around the edge of her drum-shaped farthingale. Women's dresses, as portrayed in paintings from the time, look as though they could stand by themselves.

Farthingales were worn in England until 1620 or so, when they went out of fashion in Puritan England. In Spain women continued to wear farthingales well into the 1600s. Gradually the shape widened from side to side and flattened out from front to back.

Elizabeth also expected the men in her court to look fashionable at all times. If anything, men's fashions were more outrageous than women's. Fortunes were spent on (and drained by) wardrobes.

What did men wear? What had been in vogue during the reign of her father, Henry VIII—huge shoulders, bulging sleeves, and brightly ornamented codpiece—deflated in most aspects into a distinctly feminine look. Men wore corsetlike bodices, slimmer-shouldered doublets, puffed sleeves, lacy ruffles, frills, jewels, perfume, ruff collars, and high heels. They even took to padding the fronts of their doublets in a bizarre style called a "peascod belly" that made them look paunchy. The doublets were stuffed with "bombast," which could be rags, horsehair, sawdust, or grain.

Portrait painters from this period understood the importance of paying careful attention to how they painted a person's clothing and accessories, which were meant to show off wealth and status.

Their lower garments ballooned out and were called "melons" or "pumpkin breeches," which might

WHAT Now?

BOMBASTIC: Nowadays it means "inflated" or "pretentious" or "pompous." Can you see how "bombast" is at the root of this modern adjective?

FRILLY BUT Fierce

ROBERT DEVEREUX, EARL OF ESSEX

Devereux wears white, the color of faith and humility. He would later wear red, the color of courage, to his execution on the chopping block.

69

also be stuffed with bombast. Ruffs extended far beyond the shoulders, pinned to a wire frame and tilted at an angle. Courtiers often purposefully slashed the surfaces of their clothes to show the contrasting color underneath.

The extreme fashions during Elizabeth's reign weren't worn only by the aristocracy. Even the working woman wore a stiffened bodice. If she couldn't afford a farthingale, a fashion-conscious woman managed to achieve the effect of a skirt that widened at the hips with a "bum roll" tied around her hips underneath her petticoat.

The working man wore a jerkin (vest) or a doublet (jacket). Working men's jerkins were usually made of leather. On his lower half he might wear baggy breeches, or, if he wanted to show off his legs,

balloony breeches that ended anywhere from the crotch down to the knee. Working men would have worn woolen hose (tights), which had to be held up with garters (knitted ties around his thighs).

No one wore underwear. Men's shirts were long and tucked up and under. Women wore a smock or chemise of linen. These linen undershirts doubled as nightwear.

In the days when bathing was infrequent or nonexistent, people kept their underclothes relatively clean. The idea was not to promote hygiene necessarily—it was more to protect one's outer clothing from one's oily, dirty, grimy body.

Most European and American women would not start wearing underwear until the 19th century (see I See Muslin, I See France, page 111).

In spite of the lacy, feminine dress men wore, a violent streak ran through 16th-century English society. Everyone carried a dagger. Murders were common, punishments severe, and swashbuckling adventurers risked life and limb for their queen—all while wearing perfume, makeup, and high heels.

Two of Elizabeth's most famous male subjects (and distant relatives of one another)—Sir Walter Raleigh and Sir Francis Drake—epitomized the contradictions in the Renaissance male.

Before Queen Elizabeth assumed the throne (in 1558), Spain and England had been allies for many years. Spain was the most powerful nation on Earth, while England was deeply in debt. Relations chilled between Catholic Spain and the new Protestant English queen when English ships entered territories that the pope had declared belonged to Spain and Portugal and began trading—namely, the New World, Africa, and Asia. Raleigh and Drake raided Spanish ships laden with silver, gold, and cochineal (see Seeing Red, page 54), greatly enriching the English crown. To the English, they were gentleman-adventurers. To the Spanish, they were just pirates.

Many people know Sir Walter Raleigh (1554–1618) as the courtly gentleman who spread his cloak over a puddle so Queen Elizabeth would not dirty her shoes. It's uncertain whether this actually happened, but even if the story is true, his cloak was most likely made of leather and easily cleaned. But Raleigh did a lot more than show concern for the state of Queen Bess's footwear.

Standing nearly six feet (1.8 m) tall, handsome, and a lover of fine clothing, Raleigh was also a writer, adventurer, poet, sailor, and favorite of the queen.

Raleigh tried twice to find the fabled El Dorado, a city in the New World that Europeans believed was paved with gold. Between 1584 and 1589 he organized several expeditions to North America and staked a claim for England, calling the new colony on Roanoke Island "Virginia" after Elizabeth, the virgin queen. (The colony later mysteriously disappeared.) Although his colonies were not successful, his many raids against the Spanish were quite profitable for England. Raleigh fell out of favor with Elizabeth's successor, James I. In 1618 he was beheaded for attacking the Spanish (who had once again become allies of England).

SEA CAPTAIN or Pirate?

DEPENDS ON WHOM YOU ASK. Sir Francis Drake (1540–1596) was an accomplished navigator who sailed around the world. He was also a slave trader. And he regularly attacked Spanish ships and stole the goods they carried.

In order to understand why the queen knighted Drake, it's important to understand that the English and Spanish were archenemies. In the rush to explore the New World (and grow rich plundering the wealth found there), the British and Spanish were fierce rivals. Elizabeth considered it fair game for Drake to attack and plunder Spanish ships. After all, the Spanish had stolen the stuff from the Aztec. Drake simply restole it from the Spanish.

RUFF TIMES

Jamestown colony, Virginia – early 1600s

Of the approximately 6,000 people who came from England to settle in Virginia between 1607 and 1624, only about 1,200 survived. They died of starvation, disease, drought, and attacks by Indians.

During the bitter winter of 1609–1610, the starving settlers in the Jamestown colony ate cats, dogs, rats, and even snakes to stay alive. After that they made a porridge by boiling their ruff collars, which had been stiffened with flour-based starch.

BOWING & SCRAPING

DRESSED TO IMPRESS

Royal courts, Europe, 1400s – 1800s

Fashion has dictated the proper way for a man to bow: He should bend from the waist. Historically, it was hard to do much else if you were wearing a tight corset. Similarly, a woman's careless curtsy could result in a shower of pins if she weren't careful. Not only would she be wearing a corset, but with her overskirt painstakingly pinned to her farthingale or crinoline, the most prudent way to curtsy was to sink down slowly, vertically, and cautiously, a technique that seemed to dislodge the fewest number of pins.

Paints
& POWDERS

Makeup has been applied since ancient times, and across many cultures and for many centuries it contained corrosive, caustic, and poisonous substances. Ancient Greek and Roman women used cosmetics freely. So did the Elizabethans. Greek women achieved a pale complexion by using ceruse. The ceruse was made by steeping bars of lead in vinegar or urine and then scraping off the white powder that formed, which they mixed with egg whites, fat, or wax. Roman women used ceruse, too, and also rouged their cheeks with red lead.

During the Renaissance ceruse was freely used. When Elizabeth I assumed the throne (in 1558), the ideal of female beauty was a snow-white face, with daubs of red on each cheek. To achieve bright-white skin, women slathered white ceruse from hairline to bosom. Freckles and pockmarks from smallpox could be hidden by using a mixture containing powdered mercury. The whole surface was then spackled with egg white, which, when dried, gave the face a stiff and otherworldly sheen. One drawback was that it cracked if the wearer smiled, and turned gray after a few hours. But lighting was a lot dimmer back then.

Teeth could be painted black to mask any imperfections, and blue veins could be painted onto one's skin to make it look paler and more translucent.

After Elizabeth suffered a bout of smallpox, she began coating her face thickly with the lead paste—reputedly as much as half an inch (1.3 cm) thick in places—to smooth her pocked skin.

Another popular fad during the Renaissance was using belladonna eyedrops, made from the deadly nightshade plant. They dilated the pupils and made the eyes sparkle.

Unfortunately, ceruse, mercury, and deadly nightshade (which contains a substance called atropine) are poisonous. Ceruse could lead to baldness, mental problems, open sores, paralysis, and sometimes blindness and death. Mercury caused blackened teeth, an unsteady walk, and all too often, an early death (see Tough Job: Hatmaker, page 96). Atropine can also cause blindness.

Portrait of an unknown woman, about 16, with her face painted a deathly—and deadly—white.

POISONED Gloves

DURING THE RENAISSANCE

a popular method of murder was to dispatch your enemy with poisoned articles of clothing. Jeanne de Navarre (1528–1572), pictured right, was the mother of Henry of Bourbon, who would become King Henry of France. Jeanne was a Huguenot (Protestant), and she became involved in a series of power struggles with the Catholics. She died under suspicious circumstances two months before her son's wedding. Rumors circulated that Jeanne had been poisoned by the bride's mother, the Catholic queen Catherine de Médicis, who allegedly gave her a gift of perfumed, poisoned gloves.

Why would gloves be perfumed in the first place? Partly to mask one's own unwashed smell, perhaps, or the smells in the street, but also to mask the smell of the leather (see Tough Job: Tanner, page 88).

Scented gloves were known as "sweete bagges."

WHAT Now?

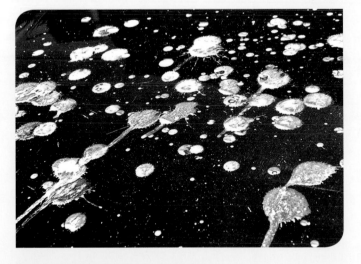

LEAD IN LIPSTICK. In 2009 the FDA found lead in nearly all samples of lipstick that it tested. The highest amounts were found in popular drugstore brands. This finding should alarm you. Because lead builds up in the body over time, years of lipstick wearing can cause unsafe exposure levels. A commonly quoted (but difficult to confirm) statistic is that women who regularly wear cosmetics "inadvertently . . . eat about 4 pounds (1.8 kg) of lipstick" in their lifetime.

Lead is also found in many nail colors and whitening toothpastes.

BIRD DROPPING FACIALS. Today many fashionable spas have begun offering these.

MERCURY IN FACE CREAMS. A study conducted by the *Chicago Tribune* in 2010 found that several skin-lightening creams on the market contained toxic doses of mercury. There's a booming market today for such creams. In some cultures, lighter skin is seen as a sign of higher status, while many lighter-skinned women use the lighteners to erase blemishes and smooth out skin tone.

In contrast to the dour Puritans, the fashion-conscious Cavaliers festooned themselves with sashes, lace, buttons, and bling.

10,000 B.C. - A.D. 1000
THE ANCIENT WORLD

1000 - 1400s
THE MIDDLE AGES

1400s - EARLY 1500s
THE AGE OF EXPLORATION

1500s - EARLY 1600s
THE RENAISSANCE

1600s - 1700s
THE AGE OF REASON

CHAPTER FIVE

THE AGE OF REASON

1600s – 1700s

LIGHTEN UP!

Putting the "Protest" in Protestant · PILGRIMS' PROGRESS · **No Rest for the Weary Colonial Woman** · THE SUN KING STRUTS HIS STUFF · **Buttons and Bows** · BIG WIGS · **What Workers Wore** · TAKE A CHAIR · **When It Rains, It Pours on You** · LEATHER REPORT · **Playing Patch-Up**

A CAVALIER

The stiff fashions of the Elizabethan period gave way to slightly more comfortable clothes by the early 1620s. In most European cities, there existed two opposing fashion trends, and the contrast was most noticeable in what men wore. On one side were the flamboyantly dressed; slouchy boots, floppy hats cocked sideways, carelessly unbuttoned jerkins—think Three Musketeers. In England these men were called Cavaliers (those who supported King Charles I in the English civil war). On the other side of the fashion spectrum were the somber Protestants of various sects—in England, there were the Puritans, and in other countries, Quakers, Baptists, Calvinists, Huguenots, and Lutherans.

For women, the prior century's artificially shaped figure—flat bosoms, stiffened V-shaped bodices, tightly pinned and drum-shaped farthingales—gave

way to a looser, rounder, more cheerful look. Paintings of this era are full of chubby cherubs and supersize nudes.

How did women achieve this new ideal shape? For starters, they ate more. Food tended to be more plentiful in many countries, so even working women who wanted to be fashionable could achieve the look. Thinner women could concoct a round abdomen by tying a "sausage roll" around their waists, under their skirts.

Following the civil war in England and the subsequent execution in 1649 of King Charles I (unpopular on several levels—among them, being an absolute monarch, being married to a Catholic, and quarreling with Parliament), England swayed far into Puritan mode. The English Commonwealth, led by Oliver Cromwell, was established, and the Puritans in charge were known as Roundheads—they cropped their hair but didn't wear wigs (see The Pilgrims, page 80).

ATTITUDE

The 1600s—a century of contrasts. CLOCKWISE FROM TOP LEFT: a Cavalier; the looser, more rounded fashion for women; a somberly dressed Puritan woman; Mr. No-Fun himself, Oliver Cromwell

THE **PILGRIMS**

DRESSED TO PROTEST

Colonial America, mid-1600s

The Pilgrims were English Puritans—not to be confused with pilgrims (see Penitents' & Pilgrims' Robes, page 36). Just to confuse you further, the Pilgrims didn't call themselves Pilgrims or pilgrims—they called themselves Separatists. They were very strict Protestants who thought the Protestant Reformation in England (1649), headed by Oliver Cromwell, wasn't strict enough. It's safe to say the Pilgrims as a group were not a cheery bunch.

They felt Cromwell's church was still too "Catholic" and that the church should enforce more austere rules of conduct. To put this view into perspective, consider that Cromwell had King Charles I beheaded, and he banned Christmas and May Day celebrations and any celebrations that involved dancing, singing, and general merrymaking. He also closed down all the theaters and urged people to dress in plain and practical clothing.

England under the "Commonwealth and free state," as it was known under Cromwell, was a dull and sober place. Interestingly, though, no laws against extravagant dress were passed. In spite of Cromwell's disapproval, some people continued to wear sumptuous clothing, patches, and low necklines.

So, the Pilgrims sailed across the Atlantic on the *Mayflower*. They landed off the coast of modern-day Massachusetts.They paved the way for thousands of others who settled in New England. By the mid-1600s there were more than 80,000 colonists living in the New World.

The early colonists wore the clothes they had brought with them from England, and for most of the 1600s and 1700s, up until the Revolutionary War, people relied on textiles imported from England. These ranged from coarse linens to fine silks (cotton from India was rare and expensive at the time). The British government controlled colonial textile production, fearing it would compete with British manufacturers (see Getting Pelted, page 95).

As we know by now, people's outer clothing was rarely washable. But the shirts and chemises people wore next to their skin were washable.

Still, laundry was an ordeal, as there was no such thing as laundry soap back then. The colonial wife used a smelly combination of wood ash, animal fat, and lye. Every garment had to be boiled, scrubbed, pounded, and dried by hand.

While outer garments tended to be imported, many colonists grew their own flax and spun and wove it into linen (see Tough Job: Flax Retter, page 13). Women and girls usually made undergarments, shirts, linens, baby clothes, and aprons. Making the cloth and then sewing the garments were just some of the hundred tasks colonial women performed. No wonder clothing was so precious. Sewing was slow and tedious work, as the sewing machine had not yet been invented (see Invention That Changed the World, Sewing Machine, page 129).

Doing laundry was just one of the many backbreaking chores of the colonial woman.

GOING FOR
baroque

DRESSED TO IMPRESS

France, England, mid- to late 1600s

Meanwhile, back across the Atlantic ...

After Cromwell's death and the restoration of the English monarchy, Charles II returned from exile at the French court and resumed the English throne in 1660. Opulent fashions came back in style, which surprised no one, as Charles and the French king, Louis XIV, were cousins. Over in France, opulent fashion had never gone out of style.

Louis XIV's court became the center of fashion, art, and culture. For women, the relatively comfy fashions of the previous decades shifted back to being impractical, uncomfortable, and unlaunderable. At least farthingales and ruffs were out of fashion (except for the Dutch, who preferred a curious, outmoded style of opulence). Skirts narrowed and collars drooped. Waists were once again boned and tightly laced, and some women took to wearing an overskirt so long it had to be carried by a page.

Men's court fashion was even more frivolous and gussied up than women's. Men festooned themselves with frills, lacy sleeves, embroidered cloth, ribbons, ostrich-plumed hats, high heels, and flowing wigs. Louis himself favored silk stockings and high-heeled shoes. Because he was only around five feet four inches (1.7 m), his high heels and high wigs helped increase his height.

Both men and women wore lots of makeup, including the time-honored and still poisonous lead ceruse (see Paints & Powders, page 73).

Under Louis XIV the French became leaders of fashion. Many people believe they still are.

King Louis XIV (seated) poses with his heirs and the royal governess. Notice how both of the standing men keep their hats tucked under their arms—hats would not have stayed put atop those huge full-bottomed wigs. The child in the dress is a boy, the future King Louis XV. The other heirs died in a measles epidemic.

Men's court fashion

WAS EVEN MORE FRIVOLOUS AND GUSSIED UP THAN WOMEN'S.

WIGGED OUT

France, England, 1600s

When the French king Louis XIV began losing his hair, wigs became fashionable at the French court. In 1660 King Charles II of England introduced wigs to his court, and few men would be seen in public without one. Periwigs, as they were known in England, were masses of curls, which often cascaded below the shoulders. The style went through several variations until by the end of the 1600s the hair (still below shoulder length) was swept upward into two peaks at either side of a center part. Luckily ruff collars had gone out of fashion—they would have severely impeded that 17th-century flow.

The fashion for wearing wigs spread, and men of nearly every social class wore them, even though wigs could be very expensive. Poorer men wore wigs of goat's hair or wool. If a man couldn't afford a wig, he arranged his natural hair so that it looked like one.

They also had to be powdered white for formal occasions. This meant sitting in your powder room draped in a cape, with a cone to your face, and getting billows of wheat starch pumped onto your oiled wig by your servant. If you had no powder room, your wig could be sent out to the wigmaker to be powdered—but you'd better have a backup.

Wig stealing became a common street crime. One tactic of a wig thief was to approach the wig wearer from behind while carrying a basket on one shoulder. Inside the basket, a small child would be crouching. As the thief approached the victim, the child would snatch the wig from the wearer's head and then

In the late 17th century elaborate, intricately curled wigs often reached all the way down to the waist. It was perfectly acceptable to comb your wig in public.

crouch back down into the basket. Because the wigs itched, men who wore wigs often shaved their heads, and so they were left embarrassingly bald when their wigs were snatched. (This may have been why so many people wore nightcaps to bed—to keep shaved heads warm.)

Wigs went out of fashion for a while when the plague struck London in 1665. Men took to wearing their natural hair, as people feared—often correctly—that the hair of the wigs had been snipped from the heads of dead plague victims. But the fashion for wigs returned after the plague had passed.

By the beginning of the 18th century, wigs for men throughout much of Europe transformed from the "full-bottomed" wig to a lighter, easier style. It's the one we associate with the Founding Fathers—a sausage roll of curls over each ear, and a short ponytail in the back. By the middle of the 18th century, even servants could afford wigs.

WORKING WEAR

England, 1600s

Clothing was such an investment that even better-off people tried to refresh their worn clothing by mending, scouring, turning inside out, restitching, and dyeing their garments. But when something got too worn to wear, it was usually passed on to servants. By the time clothing had been taken to the used clothing vendors, it had been worn two, three, or four times over. And it was to the used clothing vendors that many working people went to buy their clothes. Clothes from these vendors tended to be hard, stained, stiff, and smelly.

Even so, many of the working poor did what they could to mend, patch, and alter their used garments. Sometimes they took them to a "botcher" for repairs. The wife of an 18th-century botcher complained of being surrounded by "nitty coats and stinking hose."

ABOVE: Working men, like the farmers in this painting, wore sturdy jackets—called doublets—usually made of canvas or wool. BELOW: A Dutch kitchen maid wears a white linen cap and a white smock under her stiffened bodice in this 1646 painting.

PROTECTIVE Footwear

IN ADDITION TO THEIR APPALLING FILTH, city streets could be extremely hazardous in wet or icy weather. As rubber hadn't been invented yet, shoes had no rubber soles to grip the slippery surfaces. Wealthy people wore galoshes, a sort of protective overshoe made of wood or leather. Or they slipped their delicate footwear into sturdy pattens, which were wooden platform overshoes that could raise the wearer above the worst of the muck.

You wonder how often people like milkmaids, water carriers, and sedan chairmen lost their footing in their inadequate and ill-fitting footwear. As shoes didn't yet come with a right foot and a left foot, wipeouts, chafing, and blisters must have been a big problem (see If the Shoe Fits, page 141).

JAPANESE Style

THE JAPANESE VERSION of the patten was called a *geta* (a wooden clog elevated on two flat wooden slats).

Nobles wore getas that were 10 to 12 inches (25.4–30.5 cm) high, not only to stay out of the worst of the mud, but also to raise themselves above common people.

SEDAN CHAIRS

DRESSED TO BE SCHLEPPED

Europe, 1600s

How did people manage to keep their clothes clean before the concept of "machine washable" existed?

Well, most people didn't. If you owned only one set of clothes, as most working people in the Western world did, it wasn't easy to remain presentable while washing your one outfit.

But even for well-off people who did own several sets of clothing, keeping one's clothes clean could be a real challenge. Working women's hemlines tended to be somewhat shorter than those of wealthier women, which made walking through the streets easier (something wealthy women rarely did). Most women raised their petticoats above the muck when crossing the streets (but in some cities it was considered improper to show even a glimpse of ankle). And everyone knew enough to stay alert for people calling "gardyloo!" from upper-story windows—that warning cry meant someone was about to dump the contents of his chamber pot into the street below.

Most fabrics were not colorfast (see Hygiene and History, page 100), and before umbrellas or raincoats were invented, the colors could run badly if you were caught in a rain shower. Rain also created muddy ruts in the roads.

To preserve their fine clothing, many Londoners chose to travel by hackney—a hired coach pulled by horses. But coaches didn't guarantee you'd arrive somewhere clean. The four-wheeled coaches pulled by two horses quickly became known as hackney hell carts because of the drivers' reckless navigating.

Most 17th-century city streets were too narrow for a large coach anyway. So people who could afford to hired a sedan chair.

First introduced to England from Italy in 1634, a sedan chair was a boxlike compartment suspended between two long poles. The chair was carried through the streets by two porters, called chairmen, one in front, one in back. The chair could be carried right into the house, where a person in fine clothing would enter it and then be transported through the narrow, filthy streets without so much as setting foot outside. The poles were long and rather bouncy, and running through crowded streets involved a great deal of stopping, starting, and quick maneuvers, so riding inside these compartments must have resulted in a whole new level of teeth-jarring motion sickness. Sedan chairmen wore thick overcoats to try to protect themselves from frequent downpours.

TOUGH JOB: Tanner

PRESERVING AND SOFTENING animal hides and turning them into leather and suede is a smelly, complicated process that has been around since ancient times. Tanners steeped the hides in pits filled with caustic substances, to loosen the hair and soften up the tissues. After a few weeks, the gently softened and very slimy hides were then scraped of their rotted flesh. The hair was smeared with dog poop (which contains a softening enzyme). If you can stand to read more—the mixture was then heated up, to speed the softening process. Hard to imagine what the neighborhood must have smelled like. This was highly skilled labor, but it gave off revolting fumes, and the caustic chemicals tanners used caused serious long-term health problems.

UMBRELLAS WEREN'T INTRODUCED to England—one of the rainiest climates in the Western world—until the 1660s, but even then they didn't catch on. They also appeared in the French court of Louis XIII, but were most likely nonfolding wooden frames covered with oiled and waxed cloth. Folding umbrellas appeared in Paris in 1715. For a while, men didn't deign to carry umbrellas, because to carry one suggested that you weren't able to afford a horse-drawn carriage. It's a wonder they took so long to catch on, considering that almost no fine fabrics were colorfast, and a few drops of water could stain fine silk or satin. It wasn't until the 19th century that people began to appreciate the appeal of keeping their clothing dry.

In 1806 an average umbrella weighed about ten pounds (4.5 kg).

In England umbrellas were black, so the sooty air wouldn't stain them.

DRY CLEANING
(THE ORIGINAL METHOD)

DRESSED TO FUNCTION

Europe, 1600s

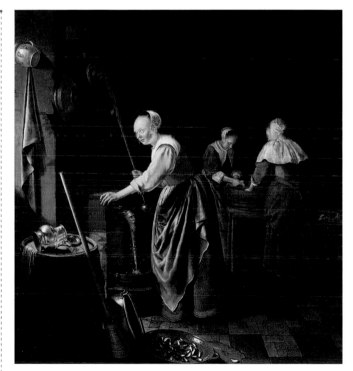

Judging from the fact that good personal hygiene was not a top priority at any social level during the 16th and 17th centuries, most people were probably a good deal more tolerant of smelly and soiled clothing than we are today. But if your clothing got especially dirty—say, your pattens slipped out from under you and you landed in a pile of poop—you could always employ dry cleaners to remove spots and stains from your fine clothes.

How did they get the dirt out? Soap made from lye, a smelly concoction made of ashes and animal fat, had been around since the 1450s, and it worked on underclothes reasonably well. Laundresses might also smear the clothing with mud or with dung, which is why so many chemises were then doused with perfume.

But harsh scouring wasn't a good option for very fine fabrics. Most cleaning methods for clothes consisted of rubbing, beating out, and airing. Other cleaning methods included "dry scouring" (vigorously brushing) or first applying any number of stain removers—such as fuller's earth (a type of absorbent clay), turpentine, rock alum, white wine, vinegar, gin, butter, or new-laid eggs—and then vigorously brushing.

PATCHING
THINGS UP

France, England, 1600s – 1700s

What was the must-have accessory for the style-conscious French courtier of the 17th century? Patches. Patches were made of black velvet, silk, or leather and were often cut into whimsical shapes like stars, circles, hearts, and moons. People stuck them to their faces with a sticky tree sap called gum mastic.

Both men and women wore patches. Smallpox, syphilis, and other dreaded diseases could leave the skin blemished, pitted, and permanently scarred, and patches could cover up the worst of the damage. But as the patch fad swept through France and other parts of Europe, people wore them to send messages. A woman wore a patch on her right cheek to let people know she was married. A patch near the mouth signified that a young woman was available for wooing. In England, at the height of the fad, members of one political party wore their patches on the left; another party wore them on the right. People carried around small boxes with extra patches in case one fell off, or to change them over the course of an evening, according to their whim.

Patch wearing persisted for nearly 200 years. The craze declined by the end of the 18th century, coinciding with the introduction in 1798 of the smallpox vaccine, which led to a vast decrease in scarred and pitted faces in need of cover-up.

PATCH BOX

Patches could be used to cover smallpox scars, lesions from syphilis, or, in the case of Peter Mews (pictured), larger imperfections. He was wounded in the face in a battle in 1685.

A scene depicting the French Revolution's Reign of Terror (1793–1794). French aristocrats on their way to the guillotine are surrounded by jeering mobs.

10,000 B.C. - A.D. 1000

1000 - 1400s
THE MIDDLE AGES

1400s - EARLY 1500s
THE AGE OF EXPLORATION

1500s - EARLY 1600s
THE RENAISSANCE

1600s - 1700s
THE AGE OF REASON

MID-1600s - EARLY 1800s

CHAPTER SIX

REVOLUTIONARY TIMES

METHODS · METHODS

HATS
(AND HEADS)
OFF

Elaborate 18th-century hats, probably all made from beaver pelts. Clockwise from upper left: "Crossing a Dirty Street," 18th century; portrait of a baron, 1710; portrait of a knight of the Constantinian Order; Portrait of Lady Worsley, circa late 1700s.

GETTING
Pelted

ALL THE RAGE

North America, 17th century

Europeans who sailed to the New World in the 17th century arrived to find a vast, uncharted wilderness. Most settled near rivers along the Atlantic coastline, where they could have access to ships and supplies arriving from Europe. But some brave explorers left the relative safety of the settlements to travel to unknown (to Europeans) territories to the north and west. What prompted early adventurers to leave the colonies, enduring harsh weather, hostile natives, scant food, and grueling travel conditions? Were they in search of fame? Gold? Honor? Land?

None of the above. They wanted hats.

Or at least, they wanted to make their fortune in the hat trade. Everyone wore hats in those days. And hats made from beaver pelts (skins) were considered the best kind of hat. A beaver hat could last a lifetime. Many men willed their hats to their sons. The demand for beaver hats came from all corners of Europe and as far away as China. English Puritans wore stiff, cylindrical black hats—think Pilgrims, since that style crossed to America with the *Mayflower*. The French chevaliers (think Three Musketeers) wore

soft, low-crowned hats with wide brims, with or without an ostrich feather, and the bourgeois burghers wore high-crowned hats with foxtail plumes. The Dutch Calvinists wore tall, severe hats to go with their outmoded white ruff collars.

In many 17th-century societies, the shape and style of your hat announced your profession, social ranking, and wealth. And everyone knew what your hat meant.

Why was beaver the most sought-after hat material of the 17th century? Felt made from beaver fur could hold its shape, even through repeated soakings in rainy European climates.

French Huguenots were highly skilled workers, employed mostly in the textile trades. They knew the secret to the process of turning beaver pelts into the felt used to make beaver hats. Huguenots were also Protestants, during a time of widespread religious intolerance. In very Catholic 17th-century France, it was growing increasingly unsafe to be a Protestant.

The thriving trade between Europeans and Native Americans was a win-win for both sides, at first.

For a time the Huguenots had enjoyed a wary but tolerable coexistence with French Catholics, thanks to the Edict of Nantes of 1598, which had been issued by the French king Henry IV. Under the edict, French Protestants had been granted freedom of worship and other civil liberties.

The Huguenots encountered increasing intolerance of their religion as the 17th century went on, and things went from bad to worse when Louis XIV decided in 1685 to revoke the Edict of Nantes. This decision turned out to be a very bad tactical error on the king's part, from a business standpoint. A bloody massacre ensued, and facing ongoing persecution, the Huguenots fled France by the hundreds of thousands. Most of the Huguenots went to England.

The sudden departure of a huge portion of France's highly skilled textile workers devastated the French economy. Not coincidentally, England's textile industry soon thrived. By the end of the 17th century, the French were reluctantly importing their beaver hats from England.

The problem was, the population of beavers across Europe had been decimated by the centuries-old demand for their pelts. By the latter part of the 1600s, it became as difficult to find a beaver left living in Europe as it was to find a Huguenot left living in France.

Luckily for the hat-fanciers, though not for the beavers, the depletion of the beaver population in Europe coincided with the discovery that beavers were plentiful in North America. The felt hat industry became a major driving force behind exploring unknown territories in the New World. Hats were one reason why England and the other major European powers bothered to establish new colonies.

Many of the adventurers did no trapping of beavers at all. They simply ventured into Indian territory and traded steel knives, tin bowls, blankets, axes, textiles, and cooking pots with the Algonquin,

TOUGH JOB: Hatmaker

HATMAKERS knew that the best beaver felts came from worn, greasy skins—and these came from Indian trappers who had tanned their pelts by pounding animal fat, liver, and animal brains into them so that they were nice and soft and greasy (see Tough Job: Tanner, page 88). The hatmaker soaked the pelt, often in noxious chemicals that included mercury. The pelt was then mashed, pounded, rolled, and immersed in a boiling acid solution to thicken and harden it. Finally, the hatter steamed the hat into shape and ironed it. Once the hat was stiffened, the hatter curled the brim into shape.

Mercury is highly toxic and can cause blackening of teeth, erratic behavior, and personality changes (see Paints & Powders, page 73). Mercury-poisoned hatters haunted many European and North American towns and cities. It could be difficult to distinguish them from drunks or madmen. Hence the origin of the phrase "mad as a hatter."

Cree, Micmac, and other tribes who lived in the forests of what is now eastern Canada.

Unfortunately, the Europeans introduced something else besides shiny new trinkets into Native American societies: disease. Lacking immunity to many Old World diseases, the Native Americans were decimated by smallpox, chicken pox, influenza, tertian malaria, diphtheria, and typhus.

By the early 1700s hatmaking had become a big business in the Colonies. Hats were one of the first American products to make England realize how powerful the Colonies were becoming. English hatters were losing a lot of customers to colonial hatmakers. England responded by passing the Hat Act of 1732, which severely restricted the manufacture and export of finished hats from the Colonies. The British wanted to import the raw materials but not the finished products. As a consequence, colonists were forced to buy imported hats made in England, from pelts exported from North America. Hats and cloth from Britain cost four times as much as locally made goods. This situation outraged the colonists, and added to their growing indignation toward England.

EXPLORATION & EXPLOITATION

DRESSED TO CONQUER

India, 1600 – 1800

Indian textile makers grew famous around the world during the 15th century for their masterful dyeing technique, especially indigo blue and madder red.

India started trading in earnest with Europeans during the Mughal period (which began in 1526). Mughal is the Persian form of Mongol—they were descended from the Mongol invaders.

But a barrier to trade existed between India and Europe—namely, the continent of Africa, which had to be sailed around in order to reach India from Europe. That's why Columbus's voyage to the New World in 1492 caused such a stir. Everyone—including Columbus—thought he'd found a western passage to India. In fact, while heading in that direction, he'd bumped into another continent—North America—which lay between Europe and Asia (see Seeing Red, page 54). Eventually the Europeans had it all sorted out, and the British, Dutch, and Portuguese established trading posts on both coastlines of India. They were joined in the 17th century by the Danes, Austrians, and French.

INDIGO Production

THE INDIGO PLANT (*Indigofera tinctoria*) is a shrub that originated in southern Asia. In the 1500s indigo was imported to Europe from India by way of Dutch, Portuguese, and English traders. It replaced woad as a cheaper source of blue dye. During the 1600s settlers in the American Colonies planted indigo.

THE COTTON Craze

DRESSED TO CONQUER

India, Europe, North America, 1700s

OPPOSITE: The Portuguese explorer Vasco da Gama is depicted showing uncharacteristic deference to an Indian raja. TOP: Weighing cotton for the British in Bombay (now known as Mumbai). ABOVE: Cotton dresses like this one became highly fashionable in the second half of the 18th century.

Thanks in part to the cottons produced in India—muslins, gauzes, and lawns—cotton became hugely popular in the second half of the 18th century. It was relatively cheap, comfortable—and washable. Indian cotton was far superior to anything produced in the West. So British manufacturers carefully studied Indian weaving, dyeing, and printing techniques and copied them. By the early 1800s English manufacturers were able to produce cloth of similar quality to India's.

INVENTION THAT CHANGED THE WORLD

COTTON Gin

IN 1793 ELI WHITNEY INVENTED the cotton gin, a machine that removed the cotton fiber from the seeds. The United States became a leading producer of raw cotton, outstripping India and Egypt. Whitney's invention revolutionized the U.S. cotton industry and made many cotton plantation owners in the South wealthy. But it also led to an increased demand for slave labor in the fields (because picking cotton is extremely labor-intensive), and for child labor in the booming cotton mills.

HYGIENE and History

ONE REASON Indian cotton was so popular was that colors on it didn't run when they got wet. Think about this. Europeans had been wearing colored cloth for centuries that couldn't be washed—at all. Even a few drops of rain could spot fine velvets and silks. (See also Umbrellas, page 89.)

The Indians possessed knowledge of dyeing with a unique use of mordants—those are the chemicals that fix the color of a dye and prevent it from running. So we have Indian dyeing techniques to thank for a big boost in the level of public hygiene in the West. For the first time, people could actually launder their clothing.

Unfortunately, the West's demand for cotton created a sinister, "triangular trade." Ships full of cotton cloth left Europe—primarily from Britain, the world leader in the cotton-textile industry—and arrived in Africa. There, British and European merchants traded their textiles and other manufactured goods for slaves. The slaves were then transported to North America and traded in the West Indies for sugar and rum, and to the southern Colonies of America for raw cotton, indigo, and tobacco. The ships returned to England and Europe, where the raw materials could be turned into finished cloth. Britain grew wealthy on this triangular trade. By the 1830s cotton goods made up half of Britain's exports (see The Signers of the Declaration, page 106).

ABOVE: Boats loaded with cotton on the Ganges River in India, 1860s
OPPOSITE (LEFT): A Russian cartoon depicts Peter the Great as a barber attempting to "westernize" his subjects.

PETER THE GREAT

PETER THE GREAT'S REIGN

WHAT NOT TO WEAR (TRADITIONAL DRESS)

Russia, 1672 – 1725

Peter the Great, so named because he was nearly six feet seven inches (2 m) tall, became tsar of Russia in 1682. He set about forcing his subjects to drop their old, Asiatic ways and become more westernized. He wanted his new city, St. Petersburg (named after himself), to be perceived as a European capital, so he had it built facing toward the West. He died before it was fully completed.

Eager to emulate his contemporary, Louis XIV of France, Peter insisted that his nobles dress like Europeans. He abolished traditional Russian garb—long caftans, fur jackets, baggy trousers, and floppy boots. Instead he insisted on tailored jackets and tight breeches. He also decreed that men must shave their beards. He thought they looked old-fashioned. Those who did not shave had to pay a heavy tax. Many opted to pay to keep their beards, which had long been a sacred tradition in Russia. Others secretly kept their cut-off beards in order to be buried with them.

GO, DOG, GO (AWAY)!

DRESSED TO PROTECT

Europe, American Colonies, 1700s

It's hard for those of us living in modern-day towns and cities to imagine just how filthy and chaotic most streets were in the days before modern sanitation systems had been built. In addition to the noise and filth and traffic, another menace plagued pedestrians: roving packs of dogs.

Back in the 18th century, rabies was a real threat. Louis Pasteur wouldn't discover a vaccine until late in the 19th century. The dog menace probably prompted the fashion for otherwise able-bodied gentlemen to carry walking sticks and canes. Sticks and canes came in handy for whacking away attacking canines. (Later, umbrellas probably served a similar function.)

FLOWER IN THE Buttonhole

IT'S A QUAINT TRADITION, watching your older sister, or your older brother's date, try not to mortally wound her prom date as she fastens on a boutonniere. The flower in the buttonhole tradition began in 18th-century France when French noblemen stuck flowers in the buttonholes of their waistcoats. The flowers served a very real purpose back then, as the wearer could remove the flower and hold it under his nose when passing through smelly corridors or streets.

RUNNING FOOTMEN

DRESSED TO SCHLEP

Europe, 1600 – early 1800s

"Make way!" "By your leave, Sir!" came the warning shouts that added to the already nerve-jangling noise level of a city street back in 1700 or so. Savvy pedestrians knew enough to heed these warning shouts.

The running footman was a specialized type of servant that first appeared in Europe in the 15th century. In cities, footmen ran in front of sedan chairs, shouting at pedestrians to get out of the way. On longer journeys out of town, his job was to run in front of the carriage and be available to help steer the horses around bad roads, or lift it out of ruts. He also ran ahead to prepare an inn for his master's arrival. Footmen were often chosen more for their good looks and level of fitness than for their good character. Running footmen wore a light cap, jockey coat, white linen trousers, or just a knee-length linen shirt. They usually carried a pole six to seven feet (1.8–2.1 m) long—or, if it were nighttime, a lighted torch. On their feet they wore thin-soled shoes. In the early 1700s some wore kilts, but these had a tendency to fly up as they ran—and they wore nothing underneath.

In 1732 *Gentleman's Magazine* railed against the insolence of the footmen, chosen "for their Size, Hair, Beauty, rather than their Industry, Fidelity and Honesty." The writer went on to complain, "In the Streets we are affronted by them, while these Harbingers to the Chairmen thunder in your Ears, 'Stand by! Clear the Way!'"

By the early 19th century, as roads improved, running footmen had a hard time keeping up with carriages, and the position eventually became that of a house servant.

A running footman, depicted on a sign at a pub

I AM THE ONLY RUNNING FOOTMAN

VENICE

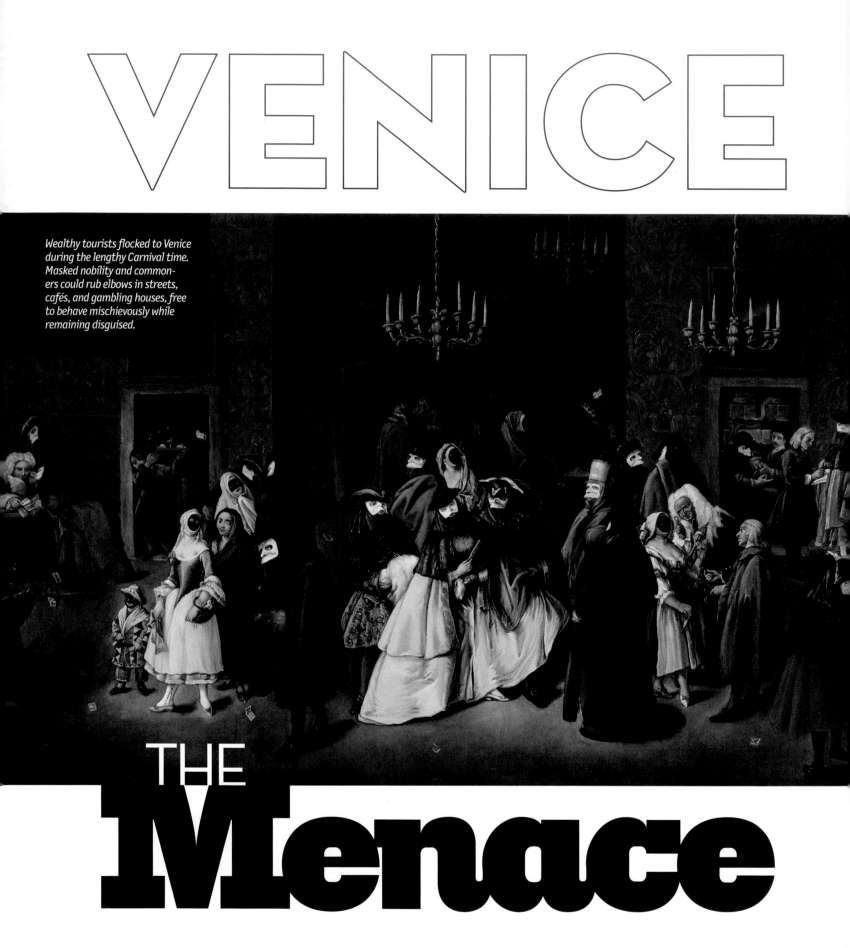

Wealthy tourists flocked to Venice during the lengthy Carnival time. Masked nobility and commoners could rub elbows in streets, cafés, and gambling houses, free to behave mischievously while remaining disguised.

THE Menace

DRESSED TO PARTY

Venice, 1600s

Masks are closely associated with the history of Venice, which is in modern-day Italy. If you were to visit that city today, you would find the place teeming with Venetian masks for sale, from the toniest boutiques to the most modest of vendor stalls.

Venice had long been a powerful commercial and naval city, but by the 18th century the city was in political and economic decline. A powerful group of wealthy families, loosely associated with the church, ruled over the citizens. The streets and cafés swarmed with spies who reported any suspicious activity to religious police.

Masks had been a feature of Venice for centuries. Wearing masks began as part of a tradition observed in many European cities. People wore masks during the week preceding Lent and leading up to "fat Tuesday" (*Mardi Gras, Martedi Grasso*), which was a time to feast and celebrate. This pre-Lent, weeklong holiday was known as Carnival (or *Carnevale*, in Italian, which means "farewell to meat").

People in Venice wore their masks for longer and longer time periods, extending from early October, all the way to March, as well as during other religious holidays and festivals over the course of the year. Gradually, most citizens of the city—men, women, children, tiny babies— spent a large part of the year in disguise.

Every night Venetians and visitors from all over the continent converged on the piazzas wearing masks and long cloaks that hid their age, rank, and identity. The masks served an important purpose to the citizens and the government alike. Every citizen could voice an opinion without fear of being punished, and spies could question people without blowing their cover as spies.

Even today, people occasionally wear masks in Venice for special occasions, including Carnival.

But people took advantage of their concealed identity. Masks were a great social leveler. Nobly born women could visit the rudest gambling establishments. Masked nuns and monks could dress up in the latest fashions and behave as immorally as their fellow citizens.

Lured by the nonstop party going on in this beautiful city, visitors from the rest of Europe flocked to Venice during Carnival season, and by the 18th century, Venice became known far and wide for its many gambling establishments, foppishly fashionable citizens, and its beautiful courtesans. Venice had redefined itself as the pleasure capital of Europe.

The Catholic Church disapproved of the immoral behavior that masking unleashed, but so long as Venetians kept sending their generous donations to Rome, the pope looked the other way.

In the late 1700s Napoleonic France became the reigning superpower of continental Europe. In 1797 Napoleon and his troops swept through Venice and occupied the city. A few months after that Napoleon signed a treaty that gave Venice and the rest of the cities of the Venetian republic to Austria, in exchange for some territories in Belgium. Under Austrian domination the wearing of masks was banned, life grew drastically less fun, and Venice's 1,100-year reign as the "queen of the Adriatic" came to an end.

The Declaration signers wearing natural, powdered hair. Homespun cloth was a sign of patriotism.

THE SIGNERS OF
THE DECLARATION

DRESSED TO PROTEST

Colonial America, 1776

John Hancock, who signed his famously large signature (so that King George could read it without his spectacles), was a wealthy man and fond of fine clothes in vivid colors. He wore a scarlet coat with ruffles on his sleeves, a white satin embroidered waistcoat, and shoes with silver buckles. On his head he wore a tricorn hat (similar to that worn by the French), and on his lower half, tightly fitting knee breeches (see Colorful Clothes and the Color of Money, page 136).

TRICORN HAT

Many of the signers of the Declaration of Independence had given up wigs, which had been popular for men in the early 1700s. Now they wore their natural hair, tied back in a ponytail, oiled, and then powdered with white flour or starch (see Wigged Out, page 84).

The tight breeches men wore led to a fashion for showing off muscular calves. If nature fell short, you could slip padding into your stockings for that shapely look. Some breeches were so tight (and this was before stretch fabric) many men took to ordering two pairs; one for formal occasions when you didn't have to sit down, another, looser-fitting pair for every day. (Thigh padding could also be purchased.)

In the time leading up to the American Revolution, wearing homespun cloth became a sign of patriotism and a symbolic protest against the Colonies' reliance on British imports. Another declaration signer, Benjamin Franklin, shocked many people in the French court of Louis XVI when he showed up to court without a sword and wearing no wig. He wore a suit of plain, dark velvet, which stood out drastically next to the lacy finery of the French courtiers. One observer wrote: "I should have taken him for a pig farmer, so great was his contrast with the other diplomats, who were all powdered, in full dress, and splashed all over with gold and ribbons." This was two years after the American War of Independence had ended, and a decade before the French Revolution. The antiroyalist message his clothes sent couldn't have been lost on the French people of the time.

YANKEE Doodle

Yankee Doodle went to town
A-riding on a pony,
Stuck a feather in his hat
And called it macaroni.

EVER WONDER what this song actually means?

When the Revolutionary War broke out, British soldiers sang the song to ridicule untrained and badly dressed American fighters. The song compared them to a certain group of foppish, perfumed young London men who dressed in lacy, frivolous fashions and were called "macaronis." The British soldiers were being ironic, as the ragtag American soldiers were dressed the opposite of a macaroni.

But the jeering song backfired. The American soldiers adopted it as their theme song, playing it on their fifes and whistling it constantly. When the British surrendered at Yorktown in 1781, the Continental Army played "Yankee Doodle" as the defeated British soldiers marched past them.

HOOP SKIRTS
(PART *DEUX*)

ALL THE RAGE

France, mid-1700s

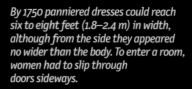

The second major appearance of hip-widening hardware occurred in the mid-1700s. These hooped petticoats would later become known as panniers (sometimes spelled "paniers"), or as "improvers" in England. By strapping these hinged, iron hoops to their hips beneath their petticoats, women could make their skirts reach truly impressive dimensions.

During the 1750s and 1760s skirts could extend from the body by more than an arm's length from side to side (try spreading out your arms and you'll see how wide that is), and as a result designers and architects were obliged to design wider chairs, doorways, and staircases. Even so, women in panniers had to slide into rooms sideways.

PLUMPERS

VIGOROUS CLEANING of one's teeth with harsh chemicals often caused people's teeth to fall out. To avoid that hollow-cheeked look, a fashion-conscious courtier could stick plumpers—cork balls—inside their cheeks. Try sticking a large round lollipop on each side of your mouth and then try speaking. That's what people sounded like.

SURVIVAL INSTINCTS

WHAT NOT TO WEAR (FANCY DRESS)

France, 1780s

During the reign of Louis XIV, French courtiers spent huge amounts of money on clothing, which financially crippled most of them. When the king died in 1715, many nobles were relieved, thinking they might get a break on their clothing budget. But no such luck. Louis XV proved just as demanding with his fashion standards. Their financial situation went from bad to worse during the reign of Louis XVI.

French fashions—particularly for women—reached an absurd extreme in Louis XVI's court. His out-of-touch, frivolous wife, Marie-Antoinette, set impossible standards. Women's hairdos reached towering heights. Hairdressers used both real and artificial hair, cemented upward over wire armatures into two-foot (0.6-m)-high coiffures. The average wig wearer towered seven and a half feet (2.3 m) tall. Their highly paid hairdressers slathered the hair with paste made from beef fat, dusted on white powder, and then added decorations ranging from stuffed dead birds to caged live birds to miniature naval warships.

To get from place to place, women had to kneel inside their carriages and lean their heads out of the windows. Because the hairdos were so time-consuming and expensive, many women kept their hair in place—and unwashed—for as long as a month. The beef-fat hair gel tended to go rancid and smell appalling, and stories circulated that not just lice but mice took up residence inside their hairdos. It was perfectly acceptable to be seen using special long wands to scratch one's scalp.

Towering hairstyles and elegant court dress quickly vanished in France after the storming of the Bastille in 1789.

MARIE-ANTOINETTE

Did bad hair days help bring on the French Revolution? In part. Dress was a highly political issue. The revolutionary leaders pointed out that flour that was used to powder the wigs of the aristocracy could have been used to make bread for the poor. Indifferent rulers, failed crops, inflation, and the bankrupt crown's overtaxation of the peasant classes brought matters to a head.

In 1789, not long after an enraged mob stormed the state prison (called the Bastille), revolutionary dress became de rigueur (considered the most judicious choice) for all classes. Alarmed nobles cast aside their finery and donned the clothes of the people, or what they hoped would pass as that. Men took off their silk heels and powdered wigs and wore riding boots and unpowdered hair, along with plain, dark blue frock coats, buff waistcoats, and long pantaloons. Ladies de-hooped themselves; removed their corsets, wigs, high heels, powder, and beauty spots; and donned wool jackets and simple muslin gowns. Most people took to wearing flat shoes, which indicated that the wearer walked rather than traveled by carriage.

The dress-down fashions adopted by members of the nobility, including the king and queen, didn't convince anyone. In 1793 Louis XVI and Marie-Antoinette were beheaded, as were hundreds of other members of the aristocracy. The enraged mobs grew increasingly frenzied, and many ordinary seamstresses, cooks, and other working-class citizens were also sent to their deaths during what

OPPOSITE, LEFT: French noblewomen wore their hair cemented over a frame, coated in beef fat, and powdered. Three-foot (0.9-m)-tall hairdos required women to sleep sitting up. OPPOSITE, RIGHT: French revolutionary colors were red, white, and blue. ABOVE: After the revolution, white muslin dresses became all the rage—even in winter. The fashion was to dress like an ancient Greek statue.

became known as the Reign of Terror.

The horrors of the revolution subsided, and by 1804 Napoleon had himself crowned emperor. The French economy was in a shambles. A neoclassical style emerged, echoing ancient Greece and Rome—thin muslin or cotton dresses that were quite impractical in the wintertime. They displayed a woman's natural shape, in an "empire" style. Waistlines rose, necklines lowered, and hair was cut short. White became the fashionable color through 1810.

But freedom to walk and breathe and bend over was not to last. Napoleon disapproved of the flimsy muslin gowns made of imported cotton. Determined to revive the flagging French textile industry, he stopped the import of British textiles and forbade women to wear the same dress more than once to court (so that they would buy more material). After the Napoleonic Wars, which ended around 1815, France's power collapsed nearly as quickly as it had risen. The British Empire emerged as the dominant power in the West. In both England and France, and soon thereafter throughout most of Europe, women's waistlines dropped and tightened, and skirts began to balloon out again. (See also Corsets, page 130.)

I See Muslin, I See France, Finally Some Underpants!

IT WAS UNDER THESE THIN, muslin, diaphanous dresses that for the first time ever, European women began wearing underwear—in the form of knee- or ankle-length drawers. In past centuries most women had worn nothing underneath besides their chemise, stays, and petticoats. Imagine wearing this kind of dress on a cold January day, before the invention of central heating. After one particularly virulent influenza epidemic carried off scores of victims in 1803, flu became known as the "muslin disease."

Why Did Napoleon Always Have His Hand in His Coat?

MANY THEORIES HAVE been proposed: He had a stomach ulcer or an itchy skin condition; he was winding his watch; he kept a nice-smelling sachet in his vest; or even that portrait painters charged extra to paint hands, to name but a few. But the probable reason is simply that it was a classic way to stand when having your portrait painted, having been established long before Napoleon's birth. Napoleon had himself painted a lot, and just made it his trademark.

More and more people streamed into cities during the 19th century, and overcrowding was most severe in the poorer neighborhoods.

10,000 B.C. - A.D. 1000

1000 - 1400s
THE MIDDLE AGES

1400s - EARLY 1500s
THE AGE OF EXPLORATION

1500s - EARLY 1600s
THE RENAISSANCE

1600s - 1700s
THE AGE OF REASON

MID-1600s - EARLY 1800s

CHAPTER SEVEN

MARCHING TOWARD MODERNITY
mid-1700s – early 1900s

GROWING PAINS

Trousers: The Long and Short of It ·
BOYS WILL BE GIRLS · **Bound and Determined** ·
Sailor Suits and Button Boots · TIES THAT
BIND · **Military Wear** · HARD TO RESIST ·
Enslaved, Enchained, Encumbered ·
MARCHING ORDERS

TROUSERS

France, early 1800s

As we know, trousers had been worn for centuries in Persia and in various regions of the Far East, as well as by working men throughout Europe. But it may have been the Battle of Waterloo (1815) that convinced fashion-conscious men in the West to give trousers a try. Both French and English cavalry soldiers wore fashionable skin-tight breeches with snazzy swallowtail coats as components of their uniforms, but their tight pants severely restricted their mobility while astride a horse, and many breeches split up the back. Soon after that, looser-fitting, long trousers replaced tight-fitting breeches, first for soldiers, and then more widely among well-dressed gentlemen everywhere.

The first trousers came with straps that buckled under the instep of the boot, so as to achieve a wrinkle-free, streamlined look. Pleats at the top helped make sitting easier, but because many men still wore corsets, toe-touching would have been quite challenging.

DRESSED TO Protest

THE LUDDITES were a group of men who named themselves after a possibly mythical figure from Robin Hood days known as Ned Ludd. The Luddites were mostly crafts-men who believed (often correctly) that the new industrial machines that were being used in the textile industry had put them out of business. They banded together in secret groups and organized expeditions to destroy them. They smashed knitting machines and industrial looms. The delicate lace-making machines could be destroyed with one wallop of a hammer. They even burned down mills. Eventually most of them were rounded up and executed.

Nowadays, the term "Luddite" has come to mean someone who stands in the way of technological progress.

CHILDREN'S Wear

Before the 18th century children of all classes dressed like their parents, in restrictive, complicated clothing (which was fussier and more complicated the higher the social status of the family).

To modern-day viewers, it might seem that all the portraits in museums painted before the 20th century that feature young children show only girls, and never boys. Every child seems to have on a frilly, flouncy dress and sport long, bouncing ringlets. But take a closer look. Many of these children are, in fact, boys. You can usually tell by the shoes—boys' heels tend to be a tad lower than those of girls, and boys tend to be painted with pet birds,

dogs, and wooden toys. Sometimes they have a tiny sword hanging across their skirt. Girls tend to be posed with dolls, feathers, and fans. For three centuries, paintings of small boys almost always showed them in ankle-length dresses. Have a look at the pictures on the right. Remember: These are all boys.

From an early age—often as young as two—girls were dressed in clothing much like their mother's. Most parents believed that a stiffened torso was essential to developing good posture, so both boys and girls were made to wear whaleboned bodices.

When a boy reached the age of six or seven he would at last discard his gown and be "breeched." The boy would don whatever was currently in fashion for adult males—in the 17th century, hose and balloony breeches; in the 18th, tight knee-length breeches; in the 19th, trousers; and, later, knickers or shorts.

The French writer Jean-Jacques Rousseau gets much of the credit for influencing the change in children's dress during the latter part of the 18th century. He maintained that children's physical and social needs were different from those of adults. Therefore, Rousseau argued, they should be allowed to wear plain, comfortable clothing. This was a radical concept for most people. "Skeleton suits" for boys appeared, so called because they fit loosely on the child's frame.

By about the 1840s boys wore high-cut trousers, short jackets, and comfortable, loose shirts, topped with natural, shoulder-length hair. Girls didn't fare quite so well in the comfort department; corsets were not discarded until well into the 19th century. Frills, lace, and ruching reemerged on girls' dresses in the mid-19th century, usually worn with thick wool stockings and side-buttoned, ankle-length boots (even in summer).

It wasn't until the end of the 19th century that girls began to wear simpler, more practical "pinafore" dresses with aprons, although always with thick black stockings, tightly buttoned boots—and woolen undergarments.

By six or seven, boys (yes, these are all boys) would discard their gowns and be "breeched."

Skeleton suits gave boys at least some relief from corsets and tight clothing.

This painting by Peter Paul Rubens of himself, his wife, and one of their five children shows the child (a boy) in a dress with a pudding cap and a leading string.

SWADDLED

HOW THEY ROLLED: Baby Wear

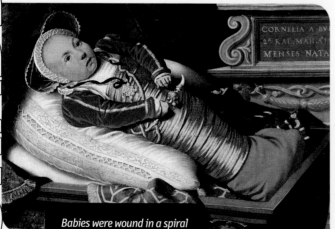

Babies were wound in a spiral bandage the length of their body for the first four to six weeks of their lives.

IN 17TH-CENTURY EUROPE AND AMERICA, babies started out life swaddled (tightly wrapped). The infant would be dressed in a shirt and tailclout (an early word for a diaper—made of cloth, of course), and then bandages would be wound in a spiraling fashion the entire length of the baby's body. On his or her head was a biggin (a cloth cap). The immobilized child might be unwound a couple of times a day to allow it to move its limbs and to be cleaned, but otherwise that's the way the baby spent the first four to six weeks of its life. People believed swaddling would give the child a straighter back and limbs.

When at last the swaddling came off, the child was short-coated, meaning it was dressed in a long, loose gown that reached to the feet. If you've ever watched a baby learning to walk, imagine adding a floor-length dress to his challenge. Toddlers could be kept out of trouble and away from blazing hearths by sewing leading strings to their clothing. The mother would hold on to one end in order to yank a child away from dangerous things like the blazing hearth, while she went about her dozens of tasks. On its head the child wore a pudding cap, which was an early incarnation of a crash helmet, with a rolled piece of fabric acting as padding if the kid fell down. Since safety pins hadn't yet been invented, baby diapers, made of linen or rags, were secured with straight pins.

By the turn of the century many boys (and even some girls) began wearing sailor suits—navy blue wool in winter, white cotton in summer. This was a pre-zipper, pre-Velcro, pre-stretch-fabric time. Getting dressed and undressed must have been an ordeal (for children as well as for their mothers or nursemaids), as everything seemed to have multiple tiny buttons.

By the time of the First World War, children's formal clothes were finally replaced by more practical garments, thanks largely to the fact that because so many servants had enlisted to serve, there were far fewer servants available to help children get their clothes on and off.

The boy is faring slightly better, comfort-wise, than the girl in this picture; she is probably wearing a corset. Their "play" scene is carefully staged for the studio photographer.

Boys SEEMED UNIVERSALLY TO hate THE FASHION.

LITTLE LORD Flaunt-Your-Boy

LITTLE LORD FAUNTLEROY, by Frances Hodgson Burnett, was published in 1886 and was an immediate hit. The book started a popular fad among middle-class women to dress their young sons, generally ages three to eight, in Fauntleroy suits of velvet, bedecked with lacy collars. Many of these boys sported flowing curls that tumbled fetchingly about their shoulders. You wonder how many boys were put to bed with their hair coiled up in rag curlers.

The suits were a status symbol for middle-class families, a visible demonstration of a family's wealth. Obviously a child dressed in expensive velvet, silk, and lace did not labor in a factory or on a farm. With the growth of the middle class, many well-to-do women had a lot of time on their hands. Many (like Burnett herself) sewed these suits for their sons themselves.

Boys seemed universally to hate the fashion.

Boys itched and sweated in their Fauntleroy suits, which, like sailor suits, shepherd's clothing, and military jackets, represented parents' fantasy roles for their children.

SLAVE CLOTHING

DRESSED TO ACQUIESCE

Southern United States, early 1800s

Many plantation owners in the southern United States imported textiles from Britain to clothe their slaves, no matter how meager were their slaves' clothing rations. "Negro cloth," as it was called, was usually a coarse, itchy wool or linen. ("Linsey-woolsey" was a combination of linen and wool.)

Male field laborers often wore knee-length linen frocks, sometimes sleeveless in the stifling heat. Women were given a scratchy shift and sometimes a petticoat (skirt).

Slave owners had a motive for dressing their slaves in similar garb. They were well aware that individuality of clothing could lead to individuality of thought and cultural identity. Some slave owners did acknowledge that permitting their slaves some variation of dress on Sundays and special holidays might raise spirits—and make them less likely to revolt. Many slaves found ways to enhance and individualize their meager clothing by dyeing the cloth bright colors from crude dyes found in nature. Red was a favorite color, whether it was a red ribbon or kerchief for a woman or a red cravat for a man.

One of the worst fates for a slave was to be sent to work in the steaming cotton and indigo fields of the Deep South. The phrase "being sold down the river" became an expression for slaves sold to planters in Louisiana and Mississippi, and widened to a more general term for being doomed to a cruel fate.

Slaves who worked in the house—butlers, maids, and personal valets—tended to get better clothing than field hands. Martha Washington's enslaved maids wore gowns of calico and linen. The livery

(servant's uniform) of male house slaves, such as footmen, waiters, and carriage drivers, was often a fine suit from a bygone era, including a coat, waistcoat, and breeches. But these dignified-looking outfits were meant to reflect the status of their owner, not the wearer. Although usually an improvement on the scratchy, inadequate clothing of field hands and other servants, these long-sleeved, heavyweight woolen liveries could be stifling in the heat of a southern climate. Both George Washington and Thomas Jefferson had liveried slaves. (See also Servant's Livery, page 143.)

Frederick Douglass, a well-known former slave who escaped to freedom and subsequently wrote a narrative of his slave days, recounted that the slave children on his plantation in eastern Maryland were allotted only two coarse, knee-length linen shirts per year.

SHAKA, Zulu CHIEF

DRESSED TO KILL

South Africa, 1820

The Zulu king Shaka (circa 1785–1828) brutally conquered and then ruled over hundreds of different communities that made up the Zulu nation. He was a born leader and a military genius, but he was also merciless and cruel when meting out punishments.

Shaka insisted that his Zulu warriors wear no footwear into battle. They practiced hardening their feet by running as much as 50 miles (80 km) a day over rough, thorny, hot terrain. In battle they wore headdresses and armbands from animal skins. Shaka and his chiefs wore leopard.

Indian mill workers carrying cotton under the watchful eye of British overseers, 1900

Cotton CLUB

DRESSED TO CONQUER

India, 1800s

After a good deal of squabbling among the various European trading companies that had established outposts in India, the British finally prevailed in the late 18th century. By the mid-19th century, the British East India Company controlled most of Europe's trade with India, generating enormous wealth both

121

By the early 1800s, the word "Manchester" became synonymous with cotton or linen. Traveling salesmen were known as "Manchester men."

for individuals and for the crown. But the company was more than just a commercial organization. It was also a military one, fighting with the Dutch, French, and members of the disintegrating Mughal Empire.

The East India Company exploited Indian subjects and forced Indian rulers to pay heavy fees for British protection. British merchants exported Indian raw materials to England, where the raw materials were turned into "Manchester cloth." The cloth was then brought back to India as finished goods and sold, driving the local weavers and craftsmen out of business. (Some was also traded for slaves in Africa; see The Cotton Craze, page 99.) In protest, many Indian people took to wearing their own homespun cloth, known as khaddar, rather than the colonial imports. British senior officers made huge fortunes. The British occupiers also failed to respect Indian traditions of religion and caste, and had almost no social contact with the millions of people whose lives they controlled. Resentment continued to build until at last, in 1857, some Indian soldiers mutinied against their British officers, which led to a full-scale Indian uprising against the British.

The mutiny was quickly suppressed. Punishments were pitiless, and the administration of India transferred from the East India Company to the

TOUGH JOB: Punkah Wallah

THE ENGLISH LIVING IN INDIA continued to wear their "respectable" Victorian fashions, which weren't well suited to the hot Indian climate, especially in an era before air conditioning was invented. Women wore corsets and long-sleeved dresses to the floor. Men wore long-sleeved jackets and trousers. Punkahs, or fans, were pulled or pumped by servants, known as punkah wallahs. The fans circulated the air over the dining room table or in the bedroom while the master was sleeping. This would have been a mind-numbingly dull task, often performed by children.

crown. India was now part of the British Empire. The British rule over India was known as the British Raj (derived from the Sanskrit word *raja,* meaning king), and Queen Victoria became Empress of India. Many Hindi and other South Asian language words entered the English language—including khaki, chintz, dungarees, taffeta, gingham, and pajamas. India did not become an independent nation until 1947, but factional troubles persisted until Mahatma Gandhi, the beloved leader, was assassinated in 1948. After that the country grew more unified.

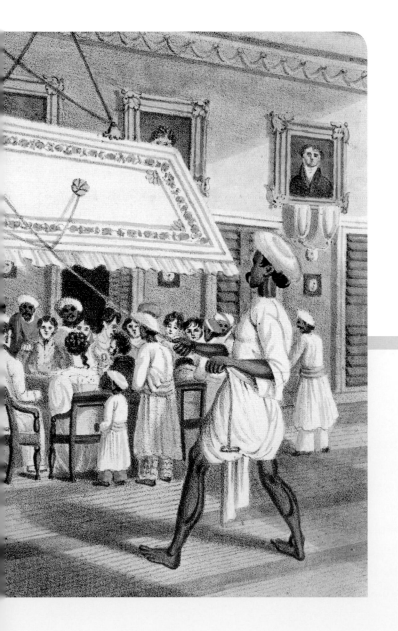

KHAKI UNIFORMS

DRESSED TO KILL

India, 1800s

In 1846 a British officer noticed that the white cotton uniforms of his Indian troops stood out as obvious targets against the dusty countryside of Peshawar (in what is now Pakistan). He permitted his troops to dye their uniforms with tea. Others may have used river mud. In any case, the camouflage helped keep them out of danger of sniper fire.

Elsewhere British soldiers continued to wear bright red uniforms well into the 19th century, often with disastrous results, as they could easily be picked off with the new long-range weapons available. Eventually British soldiers began wearing khaki uniforms for all overseas battles. Khaki comes from the Hindi word *khak,* meaning dusty. In 1898 American soldiers wore it for the first time during the Spanish-American War.

THE CHARGE OF THE LIGHT BRIGADE

DRESSED TO KILL

Russia's Black Sea, 1854

The Charge of the Light Brigade was an 1854 clash between British and Russian troops during the Crimean War. The battle has been immortalized in poems and stories as a symbol of courage and tragedy in war.

The Light Brigade was a group of well-dressed Scottish soldiers fighting for Britain. They wore kilts, bright red coats, and high fur helmets. The Light Brigade successfully defeated a charge of Russian soldiers on horseback, thanks to their use of a powerful new rifle that could be reloaded much more quickly than the old muskets. But two-thirds of the regiment was killed. The battle marked the end of splendidly-colored uniforms in combat situations. Because of the new long-range weapons available, soldiers had to make themselves less visible in order to remain safe from enemy fire.

Gandhi, after attending tea with King George V

Mohandas Gandhi (1869–1948)—popularly known as "Mahatma," which means "great soul"—took over leadership of the Indian National Congress in 1920. He led a moral crusade of peaceful resistance against British occupation and, in an effort to identify with the peasants, wore the basic loincloth of the poor. He was also pictured spinning raw cotton on an Indian spinning wheel, which became a symbol of India's fight for independence from British occupation.

In 1931 Gandhi was invited to tea in London with King George V and several hundred other dignitaries. Although the invitation called for formal dress, Gandhi showed up in a loincloth and a shawl of homespun cloth, and sandals. When asked later if he thought he had worn too little clothing, he replied, "The King had enough on for both of us."

As a symbolic gesture, Gandhi wore the clothing of poor Indian peasants and spent much of his time spinning and weaving khaddar, homespun cloth.

Mahatma GANDHI

Breaker boys, 1911, average age, eight to twelve. Their job was to sort lumps of coal by hand. They usually worked ten hours a day, six days a week.

10,000 B.C. – A.D. 1000

1000 – 1400s
THE MIDDLE AGES

1400s – EARLY 1500s
THE AGE OF EXPLORATION

1500s – EARLY 1600s
THE RENAISSANCE

1600s – 1700s
THE AGE OF REASON

MID-1600s – EARLY 1800s

CHAPTER EIGHT

THE INDUSTRIAL REVOLUTION
mid-1800s – early 1900s

LABOR PAINS

Industrial Strength · HABIT FORMING · **Shape Shifter** · HAZARDOUS HEMLINES · **Bustling Around** · JEANS AND SNEAKERS · **Dry Idea** · COLOR CRAZE · **Fade to Black** · RING LEADERS · **Body Art** · TOP HATS · **Smoker Face** · SERVANT STYLES · **Polar Opposites** · MACHINE-MADE · **Daring Swimwear** · WEDGIES · **Men in Tights** · TENNIS, ANYONE? · **Feather Frenzy** · FUR FAIL · **Dollars and Scents** · WOMEN TAKE BABY STEPS

MID-1700s – EARLY 1900s
MARCHING TOWARD MODERNITY

MID-1800s – EARLY 1900s
THE INDUSTRIAL REVOLUTION

A young spinner, 1908. The photographer Lewis Hine took many such pictures, raising public awareness and outrage.

MILL WORKERS & SWEATSHOPS

Around the same time as the French and American Revolutions, another "revolution" was unfolding. It was a time when many new technologies were discovered or improved upon, which led to huge advances in manufacturing and transportation systems. This historical period became known as the industrial revolution.

Up until the late 1700s, most machines had been powered either by water or by animals. Then inventors figured out how to harness steam as a way to power machines. This discovery caused industry to gallop forward into a new age. Powerful new machines evolved, including coal-burning engines in railways and steamships. Still others could manufacture textiles in bulk. And when the sewing machine was invented in 1846, mass production of clothing became possible.

But as mass production of clothing got better, the lives of the workers who manufactured the clothes usually grew worse.

The new industrialists built factories in the late 18th and early 19th centuries, and they employed armies of textile workers, seamstresses, and loom operators. Most of these factory workers were women and children, who could be paid a fraction of what men were paid. The working conditions could be appalling. But when workers organized and went on strike for better working conditions, they were usually fired and replaced with more recent immigrants, desperate for any kind of work. With the introduction of gaslight, long days—sometimes 17 hours—became commonplace.

The machinery was often so loud that workers had to lip-read. Many went deaf from the noise. Their lungs became so clogged with dust and cotton fibers that it was difficult to breathe, and many workers lost a finger, an arm, or a leg in the dangerous machinery. The youngest children in the cotton mill were the scavengers. Their job was to crawl beneath the spinning machines to clean up the cotton fluff that had fallen, which could ignite and cause a fire.

Sometimes whole families worked long hours from their homes, which were often situated in crowded urban slums. For a miserable wage, these milliners, dressmakers, factory girls, and freelance needle women made it possible for wealthy Victorians to dress respectably—wealthy people changed their outfits as many as six times a day.

Worse still, the raw cotton that supplied the textile industries came from the toil of slaves on plantations in the United States, or from India, which was controlled by the British East India Company and its exploitation of textile workers there (see Cotton Club, page 121).

SEWING MACHINE: 1846

INVENTION THAT CHANGED THE WORLD

WALTER HUNT AND ELIAS HOWE both figured out how to mechanize sewing, at nearly the same time. The trick was to use two threads: A needle pushed one thread into the fabric from the top while, below, a shuttle moved back and forth and looped the second thread through the top stitches. Still, it was cumbersome for the seamstress to have to stop cranking frequently while she adjusted the fabric.

In the 1850s Isaac Singer improved on the original design by developing a machine that moved along with a foot treadle. Now the seamstress had her hands free while her foot cranked the machine.

The first home sewing machines were sold in 1889. Where a man's shirt had once taken 14 hours of labor to complete, it now took about an hour and a half.

An early version of the sewing machine used small dogs to power the machine.

KICKING THE Habit

PRIOR TO THE EARLY 20th century, the only proper way for a proper woman to sit on a horse was sidesaddle. Imagine doing this while wearing a tight corset, a heavy, woolen, ankle-length skirt, and multiple petticoats. Then imagine trying not to let people glimpse your ankles.

Horses can be unpredictable. Women were sometimes thrown from the horse and dragged by their long skirts, which could be tangled in the stirrups.

All sorts of fashion solutions were invented to prevent the female rider from exposing too much scandalous ankle while sitting on the horse (still sidesaddle). Women who could afford separate attire wore special riding dresses called habits, which were longer in front and prevented exposure of the ankles.

After 1880 some women stitched an elastic tab into the hem of their dress for the foot to pass through.

Finally, thanks in part to the late 19th-century "rational dress" movement (see Bloomers, page 135), it became acceptable for women to ride cross saddle. Straddling the horse had its critics, who believed that riding cross saddle would cause girls to develop stronger, flatter thighs than nature had intended, but most women adopted the "ride-astride" costume, which was a big, divided skirt.

By 1925 it was finally acceptable for women to wear riding breeches.

CORSETS

DRESSED TO COMPRESS

United States, Europe, 1700s – 1910

The corset, that shape-shifting, organ-displacing, lung-constricting garment, first arrived on the fashion scene sometime during the 1400s. It wasn't yet called a corset, but the stiffening devices known as bodices, busks, stays, and stomachers were all parts of a kind of squeezing apparatus that reshaped the torso into unnatural configurations. The earliest corsets were stiffened with wood or whalebone. Men, women, and even nobly born children gasped and sweltered in a torso-constraining device of some sort or another.

During the Renaissance, bodices continued to be stiffened—with leather, wood, or whalebone. A flat, V-shaped board called a busk was often laced into the front of the bodice. The effect was to flatten a woman's front almost entirely.

Throughout Europe and the American Colonies, stiffened bodices or stays stayed in fashion well into the 18th century. Even the poorest women wore some form of stays. By the end of the 18th century special boned stays were designed for pregnancy, and for very young children. Many parents, obsessed with their children's posture, considered it unthinkable to allow their children—both boys and girls—to run around uncorsetted.

In the late 18th century stiffened bodices went abruptly out of fashion when revolutionary fever struck France in 1789 (see Survival Instincts, page 109). Suddenly to be tightly corsetted was a sign of aristocracy—a definite fashion don't if you wanted to avoid a trip to the guillotine. (Pictures of female revolutionaries do show that women continued to wear some sort of stiffened bodice for a while longer—poorer people couldn't afford to change their "look" as quickly as wealthier people.)

By 1825 dress waistlines were back to their natural position—and corsets came roaring back. Men still wore them, but now mostly for specialized purposes. Military men, particularly cavalry officers, wore corsets to maintain a stiff posture while mounted on a horse. Stout men wore them for vanity.

Around 1851 it finally occurred to someone to move the corset's laces from the back—which had to be pulled and tied by someone other than the wearer—to the front.

Tight lacing grew more and more severe as the waist was squeezed into an unprecedented hourglass shape, encasing the wearer from armpits to hips in an exoskeleton hard shelled enough to rival that of any crustacean.

Every activity of the wearer was affected—eating, breathing, standing, walking. Bending over was out of the question. To be flirtatious, you could drop your handkerchief in the presence of a gentleman. He'd have to be the one to pick it up—because you couldn't.

No wonder Victorian women fainted a lot. (High, tightly fitting buttoned collars didn't help much, either.)

By 1870 dresses hugged the figure closely in the front, so corsets became longer and even more constrictive, forcing the internal organs downward.

An American woman, 1899. Extremely tight corsets such as this one could exert 88 pounds (40 kg) of force on the internal organs, although most women probably didn't lace themselves this tightly.

THE **CRINOLINE CRAZE**

ALL THE RAGE

Europe, United States, mid-1800s

The crinoline (pronounced KRIN-o-lin) of the 19th century outdid its predecessors (see Frilly & Foppish, page 67, and Hoop Skirts, page 108) not just by its extraordinary size, but also by its widespread popularity among women from all social classes. First appearing around 1842, the early crinoline was a cumbersome undergarment that flared the skirt by means of whalebone, multiple petticoats, rolled fabric at the waist, and braided straw.

A respectably attired woman—including a servant girl—wouldn't think of venturing out without at least two petticoats to hide the shape of her legs. At the worst of the pre-hoop era, women staggered around wearing 15 to 20 pounds (6.8–9 kg) worth of multiple heavy petticoats. Some of these underskirts were made of stiff wool and horsehair, others boned and padded, still others starched and flounced. (And they were also wearing corsets; see Corsets, page 130.)

Women were at last relieved of much of the weight they'd been dragging around when in the 1850s a collapsible spring steel hoop crinoline was invented. Crinolines came in varied shapes and sizes, and changed their shape slightly from year to year. But all styles were some form of steel hoops of increasing diameter, attached to one another vertically by tape or ribbons. The contraptions collapsed rather ingeniously when a woman sat down, and were considered a technological marvel. In contrast to the heavy petticoats women had been lugging around, the new crinolines were light; an American version in 1862 weighed only eight ounces (0.2 kg).

All this hardware and vast quantities of dress upholstery

ABOVE AND OPPOSITE: A series of photographs from 1860, taken in a lady's dressing room, show the hoops needed to support a crinoline. In the opposite far right photo, the woman's dress is lowered over her head with the aid of long poles.

were expensive, of course, and to wear the largest crinolines required servants, who were needed to lower your gown over your cage with long poles. Women also had to live in a spacious enough house with enough open real estate to accommodate their vast circumference.

The hoops also caused big problems on trains and narrow sidewalks. To fit into the doorway of a horse-drawn omnibus, the wearer had to squeeze her skirts into an oval. One of the conductor's responsibilities was to push down on the front end of the hoop to keep the lady's dress from rising to an immodest level.

Many women took to wearing pantalettes (cotton underdrawers that tied below the knee) underneath their skirts to avoid embarrassing exposure. But it would have been virtually impossible to try to untie or pull down one's underdrawers to go to the bathroom, so women's pantalettes were crotchless.

The crinolines could also be extremely dangerous. On busy city streets, some women became entangled in the wheels of passing carriages with disastrous results. Workers who wore them in factories that made china and glassware often swept items off of shelves and broke them. Crinolines could—and often did—go up in flames if the

wearer drew too close to a fire.

What possessed women—from wealthy older women to factory girls—to wear such enormous and impractical garb? They certainly called attention to the wearer. Most likely the crinolines were worn at first by women of a high social rank as a way to stand apart, both literally and figuratively, from the common throngs. But as the craze spread rapidly to all classes, this distinction was lost.

The crinoline craze finally waned in the 1870s when the bustle (an extension of the backside) became fashionable.

SHAPESHIFTER

WHALEBONE was used as a stiffener for centuries because it was springy and flexible and kept its shape when heated and molded. In the late Middle Ages it was used to construct hennins and pointed headdresses (see Coneheads, page 49). It was ideal for boning and stiffening bodices, shaped panniers, corsets, and hooped petticoats. With the mid-1800s crinoline craze, the demand for whalebone (and for whale oil) nearly drove whales to extinction. Luckily for the whales, steel replaced whalebone as a crinoline material and as a corset stiffener. (See also Plume Fad, page 154.)

FANNY PACK—
THE
Bustle

ALL THE RAGE

Europe, United States, 1869 – 1892

The bustle made its appearance in 1869, as huge crinolines deflated and the bulk of the skirt swiveled around to the back. Bustles were padding worn beneath the skirts that made the woman's backside protrude in an extremely unnatural-looking lump. Even servant girls wore them—one lady wrote in a letter to her mother-in-law that her friend's maid pinned three feather dusters under her skirt to achieve the fashionable bump.

Bustles varied in size from year to year. Before collapsible bustles were invented, a woman who wanted to sit down pushed it a little to one side, so that "the bustle was sitting next to you on the bench." During the 1880s a "scientific" bustle was invented that could collapse when the wearer sat down and then spring back into its original shape when she stood back up.

Bustles had a distressing tendency to shift out of place under one's skirts, and must have been embarrassing to readjust in public.

Bustles could project back as far as 2 feet (0.6 m), and skirts could require 36 yards (33 m) of fabric. By the end of the 19th century a fashionable woman was lugging around 37 pounds (17 kg) of clothing.

BLOOMERS

DRESSED TO FUNCTION

England and America, 1851

An American woman named Amelia Bloomer, pictured at right, led an "anti-crinolinist" movement, which was an attempt to introduce more rational clothing for women. Bloomer was an editor of a magazine supporting women's rights. She began wearing a shocking new costume: a knee-length skirt with baggy Turkish-type trousers underneath, gathered and tied at the ankle.

To put it mildly, the look didn't catch on. Bloomers became a despised symbol of the new women's rights movement. They were thought to be an attack on the sanctity of home and hearth, and an insult to men.

Bloomers were just a little ahead of their time. Most women continued wearing long dresses for work, tennis, hiking, and the newly popular croquet (see

Athletic Wear, page 153). Many probably accepted the obvious injustice of what men could wear for sports compared to what women were expected to wear. After all, for centuries, women had been performing the extremely acrobatic and impressive feat of riding a horse sidesaddle (see Kicking the Habit, page 129). And for a good part of the 19th century, they'd been climbing mountains and crossing glaciers in crinolines, thin shoes, and silk stockings.

By the early 1900s, bloomers began to be worn as outer garments by schoolgirls in gymnasiums.

BLUE Jeans

SOME ACCOUNTS SUGGEST that the name "blue jeans" came from the French *bleu de Gênes,* meaning "blue of Genoa," a durable blend of cotton, wool, and/or silk that was used by sailors in the 16th and 17th centuries, although a similar fabric from around the same time was produced in Nimes, France, and was called *serge de Nimes* (de Nim . . .denim!). In 1853 a man named Levi Strauss left New York for San Francisco, intending to sell tent canvas to the men who had flocked west to look for gold. These gold diggers were known as prospectors. But when he got there, he learned from the prospectors what they really needed: durable pants. He had a tailor make these from his tent canvas, and they became a huge hit.

Eventually Levi Strauss reinforced the pockets with stitching so that the gold nuggets the men collected wouldn't tear the pants.

SPORT Shoes

IN 1868 a new sort of sports shoe, with sturdy rubber soles and a canvas upper, became known as a croquet sandal. The shoes were too expensive for all but the very wealthy, but the trend eventually caught on. In 1873 they were sold in the Sears catalog for 60 cents. By 1917 the first mass-marketed canvas-top, rubber-soled shoes were sold by Keds. A marketing executive dubbed them "sneakers" because the rubber sole made so little noise when walking. Two of the most famous sneaker brands, Adidas and Puma, were created as the result of a bitter feud between brothers. In 1924 two brothers from a small village in Germany, Adolf (Adi) and Rudolf Dassler, formed a sports shoe company and eventually named their shoes Adidas (after "Adi" Dassler). In 1948, after years of squabbling, Rudolf left to form his own company, which is now known as Puma.

After the invention of synthetic (aniline) dyes made bright colors available to practically everyone, dark, sober colors became the choice for the affluent.

Jean Beraud.

Western world, 1850 – 1900

By this point in the book you probably remember which colors had long been associated with wealth, power, and royalty: purple and red. These colors were the most expensive to produce, but from the beginning of human fashion history, any colorful clothes might be an indication that the person was someone of importance. During the Renaissance, dull, earth-colored clothes, derived from natural dyes, were the colors of poverty. Color was associated with high rank. The more prosperous you were, the brighter were your clothes. (True, deep black was also a status symbol, because it was difficult and costly to dye.)

During the French Revolution, wearing bright colors became unpopular, because they symbolized the aristocracy. The red tricolor hat of French revolutionaries had been dyed with French madder, rather than with expensive imported cochineal. But this anti-color period was short-lived. Bright colors reappeared during the Napoleonic period.

Why, then, the abrupt shift to darker, more sober colors during the second part of the 19th century? Ironically, it was the invention of new bright colors that led to their decline among people of means.

For men, the change happened sooner than for women. The extreme filth in urban centers probably contributed to the virtual disappearance of light-colored trousers. In most European capitals, as well as in many American cities, sunlight rarely penetrated through the dense gloom created by thousands of coal-burning chimneys. Gaslights had to be turned on by midafternoon. Add to that the filth of the streets, the horse-drawn carriages spewing mud on rainy days (or dust on dry days), and light clothing didn't stand a chance.

After 1850 men's colored coats were replaced by black ones, worn with checked trousers. The dark, three-piece suit—trousers, waistcoat (vest), and jacket—became a symbol of industrial progress.

But as men's fashions became more and more standardized, women's fashions grew more wild and varied. The rapid changes in the color of women's dresses over the course of the century have to be attributed largely to an 18-year-old chemist named William Perkin.

In 1856 Perkin accidentally discovered a synthetic dye while he was searching for a cure for malaria. The young chemist's purple-pink color, eventually called mauveine, enabled him to open his own factory in London. By 1859 the color mauve was everywhere. Perkin became a wealthy man.

Other chemists flocked to produce more colors synthetically. Two years later a magenta-colored synthetic dye was invented in France, and nearly every year after that to the end of the century, new synthetic (known as aniline) dyes were patented. For a period of about 20 years, a mania for color hit society women. Never before had colors of such unnatural intensity been seen.

As textile prices fell during the 1870s, people from nearly every income level could afford to wear

FACIAL Hair

THE LATE 19TH CENTURY

was the heyday of facial hair for men—beards, moustaches, sideburns, sometimes bushy, or twirly, or oiled. Fashionable men might also have their hair groomed and the ends of their moustaches twirled to a dastardly point with bear's grease.

WEARING White

IN THE UNITED STATES,

Labor Day has been celebrated on the first Monday of September every year since Grover Cleveland formally declared it a holiday for the working classes, in 1894.

The no-wearing-white-after-Labor-Day rule probably began at the turn of the 20th century, when newly well-to-do American families returned from their country houses to their homes in the cities, and the men returned to their jobs. It would have been out of the question to wear white in the grimy, coal-smoky urban centers.

colorful clothes. Industrial mass production had leveled the social hierarchy.

Unfortunately, some of the new synthetic dyes were made with arsenic acid, which left traces of arsenic on the textiles (see Deadly Green Arsenic, page 138). Many people, especially those who wore bright reds and greens, got rashes and developed other symptoms of mild poisoning. But the demand persisted.

After 1880 members of the wealthier classes began to view bright colors as vulgar. Except for hunting wear and military uniforms, black became the universal color for men, and more muted, less vivid colors became the fashion for "women of refinement."

DEADLY
green
ARSENIC

Europe, United States, 1700 – 1900

In the mid-1800s, most green fabric was dyed with arsenical compounds, poisonous to the wearer. Arsenical products also could help you achieve that pale, poisoned complexion.

Since ancient times, arsenic has been a favorite poison used by those wishing to get rid of someone without being caught. It's even been called "inheritance powder" for its ability to speed up the death of an impatient heir's relative. Apart from its illegal uses, arsenic was legally present in a staggering number of other areas of Victorian life. It was used as an ingredient in textile dyes, cosmetics, paint, and wallpaper. It was handy for young women, anxious to achieve the fashionable grayish/pale pallor without the use of cosmetics (considered to be improper). They ate chalk, drank vinegar, and, beginning around 1830, nibbled on arsenic wafers, which were freely marketed in many fashion magazines. These toxic wafers certainly worked, as they gave the skin a deathly, bluish tone. Sales of the product dropped off when cosmetics became more acceptable, toward the end of the century.

Green fabric became all the rage in the 1860s when aniline dyes became available (see Colorful Clothes and the Color of Money, page 136). Paris green, emerald green, emperor green, parrot green—all contained arsenic. Green wallpaper contained lethal doses, as did green gowns. In the words of one writer, "Society beauties whirling through waltzes in their green muslin ball gowns spread clouds of toxic dust like helicopters spraying pesticide."

SCARIFICATION is a custom practiced in Ethiopia and in many other nations around the world. The process involves puncturing the skin with a thorn or other sharp implement, and then rubbing ashes or charcoal into the wound, which results in a raised scar. The resulting patterns can be used as tribal markings or just to adorn the body.

OUCH!

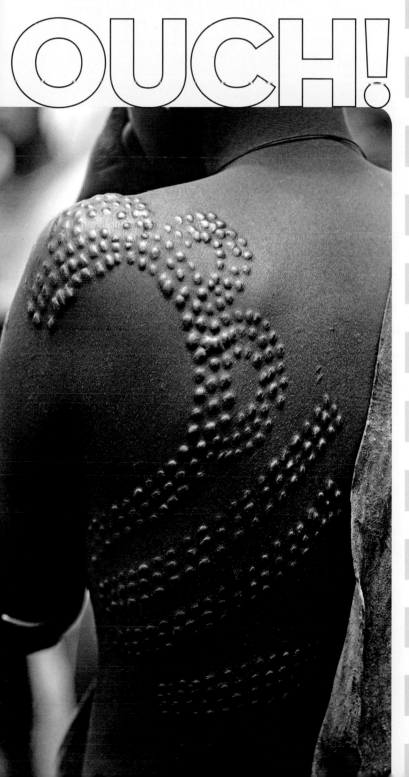

A Padaung woman with brass neck coils. They weigh about eight pounds (4 kg).

A CUSTOM AMONG THE PADAUNG TRIBE

of Burma has been to put brass neck coils around the necks of little girls from the time they are around five years old. The number of coils is slowly increased over the years until mature women may wear coils that weigh as much as 25 pounds (11.3 kg). Contrary to popular belief, the Padaung women do not have especially long necks. The coils create this illusion by pushing down on the collarbone. Women wear the coils for the rest of their lives. The coils severely restrict their ability to move their heads.

Many members of the Padaung tribe fled Burma (renamed Myanmar in 1989) because of the harsh military regime in control there, and live in Thailand, where the fashion for neck coils attracts curious tourists (and earns money for their families).

After the death of her beloved husband, Prince Albert, in 1861, Queen Victoria wore deep mourning dress for the rest of her life. Even ladies' underwear could be trimmed with black.

Women IN BLACK

DRESSED TO MOURN

England, mid-1800s

Nowadays when people attend a funeral, they don't necessarily feel they have to wear black. But it was not so long ago that people considered it unthinkable to wear anything but head-to-toe black to a funeral. "Mourning dress" was a signal to society—your clothing was a reflection of the depth of your grief.

In the 19th century "respectable" society had extremely complicated rules of etiquette about what constituted suitable dress, and mourning clothes were no exception. If a woman's husband died, she was expected to pass through three distinct phases of mourning, lasting a minimum of two and a half years. During the first phase, known as deep mourning, she was expected to drape herself in black from head to toe for 12 months and a day, preferably in black crepe, a kind of silk. If she couldn't afford a black dress, she dyed her existing dress black. The crepe was a nuisance to maintain—raindrops caused blotches on it, and if it got really wet, it could turn one's skin and underclothes black.

During the second period, which lasted for nine more months, the widow was permitted to add black silk and a few trimmings, but still nothing too shiny. By the third year of widowhood she might dress in suitable half-mourning colors, such as violet, gray, or white. This period could last from six months to the rest of her life, depend-ing on her individ-ual choice. Indoors she wore a wid-ow's cap, which could be black or white, with long streamers hanging down the back. Remarriage was frowned upon.

By 1900, the only sign that a man was in mourning was a black armband.

As for a husband whose wife had died? He was expected to wear a black armband for several months.

Although "widow's weeds" (mourning dress) were worn into the 1930s, the rules relaxed and length of time shortened after World War I, when so many families lost loved ones.

IF THE SHOE FITS ...
It must be the 19th century

BY 1865, for the first time, mass-produced shoes were made with a left and right foot. Before that, the shoes and boots made for common people were created on straight "lasts," which were not designed for right and left. People often switched their shoes around to minimize the chafing. Wealthy people who had their shoes custom made had been wearing right and left shoes since the late 18th century—before then, even fancy shoes had been "straights."

TOP Hats

MIDDLE- AND UPPER-CLASS men living in urban centers almost all wore top hats. Made of stiff canvas and covered in silk, the hats were hot and expensive and uncomfort-able. But they were a mark of respectability, a way to distinguish you from the common laborer (who wore a cap). A man's social status could be determined by the quality of his hat. Collapsible versions were worn to the opera.

England, mid-1800s

While menswear of the mid-19th century couldn't begin to rival the absurd proportions and discomfort of mid-19th-century women's wear, it was still pretty uncomfortable, and nearly always in gloomy shades of gray or black. So, in off-hours men sought comfort in a new fad: smoking jackets. These were dressing gowns, often in beautiful colored silk designs, and they became all the rage for informal dress at home. Smoking jackets enabled men to wear colors that wouldn't have been acceptable during the day. They were also a lot more comfortable than the suffocating, close-fitting costumes men wore for day. Cigarette smoking became popular, thanks to returning soldiers from the Crimean War (1853–1856) who had taken up the habit with the availability of cheap tobacco in Turkey.

Women were probably in favor of men wearing smoking jackets (known in America as robes or dressing gowns), because the smell of tobacco was hard to remove from clothes. Many men topped off the look with Turkish-looking hats, sometimes with hanging tassels.

smoking
JACKETS

SERVANT'S LIVERY

DRESSED TO SERVE

England, United States, late 1800s

The practice of dressing one's servants in sumptuous outfits from bygone eras became commonplace in upper-class homes of 19th-century London and Paris, and to a lesser extent, New York, as well as in large houses in southern states (see Slave Clothing, page 120). Nineteenth-century footmen, for example, might be dressed as 18th-century courtiers, complete with knee breeches, powdered wigs, and long, elaborately embroidered jackets in bright colors. This during an era when respectable men had taken to wearing sober, dark, three-piece suits and long trousers—bright colors and showy decorations had gone decidedly out of fashion.

Servants' clothing, called livery, could be decades out of fashion; often their masters bestowed their discarded clothing onto their inferiors. But by the 19th century it became a status symbol to dress your servants, as one writer suggests, as though they were in "the court of the decapitated Louis XVI," perhaps so that others would associate you with aristocracy and "old money," without your having to dress ostentatiously yourself.

Servants often received an outfit of clothing as part of their wages.

PANAMA Hats

PANAMA HATS are lightweight, tightly woven straw hats that are great for protecting heads from the scorching rays of the tropical sun. They're woven from a plant called *Carludovica palmata*. Despite their name, they're made not in the country of Panama, but in Ecuador. They've been made there for centuries, but the hat grew popular during the Spanish-American War in 1898, and then in 1904, with the construction of the Panama Canal, where they were worn by the construction crews.

President Theodore Roosevelt made the hat famous when he was photographed wearing his at the building site of the Panama Canal.

Matthew Henson (second from left) poses with three Inuit members of the expedition. A sled dog rests nearby.

COLD-WEATHER WEAR

North Pole, 1909

In 1886 a young naval lieutenant named Robert E. Peary walked into a hat store in Baltimore to buy himself a pith helmet. (A pith helmet is lightweight, cloth-covered, tropical headgear.) Peary was leaving for Central America on a survey trip for the government. On a whim, Peary asked the store manager if he knew of someone he might hire as a valet for the trip. The manager introduced Peary to his stock clerk, a young African American named Matthew Henson. Peary hired him on the spot. This chance encounter led to

MATTHEW HENSON

144

one of the greatest exploring partnerships in history.

In 1891 Peary received a commission from the U.S. Navy to explore and chart northern Greenland. At the time no one knew whether it was an island. Henson proved himself to be the most capable member of the expedition—he knew engineering, carpentry, and how to navigate by the stars. The team returned to the United States triumphantly, having discovered that Greenland was in fact an island and that the North Pole lay beyond it, not within it. While on the survey trip to Greenland, Henson befriended the native Inuit, who taught him their language and the skills needed to become an expert dogsled driver. They also taught him the most valuable secret of all: how to dress for the Arctic climate.

Travel conditions in the Arctic included temperatures in the minus 70°F (-56.6°C) zone, punishing winds, blinding snowstorms, and wide expanses of open water. The only way to travel was on foot or by dogsled. Padding oneself with thick layers was out of the question—it took exceptional mobility to lift sleds over blocks of ice, to climb, sled, snowshoe, and trek vast distances.

Peary wrote a book entitled *The Secrets of Polar Travel*, in which he described what an Arctic explorer must wear.

First, a skin-tight shirt of thin red flannel with a close-fitting hood, over which one wore a second thickness of flannel. Then bearskin trousers lined with flannel. Over all this they wore "a deerskin hooded coat." The face opening in the hood was made just large enough to allow the hood to be pushed back from the head in calm weather. Around this opening was a roll of soft bearskin, with only one edge sewed down; in bitter winds, this bearskin roll could be turned up like a collar to form a wind guard for the eyes and face.

On the feet were hare-skin stockings, and boots made from polar bear skin and insulated inside with dry arctic grass. Their mittens were made of bearskin, deerskin, and sealskin, and further insulated with dry grass. Remarkably, "The entire suit weighs only a few ounces over twelve pounds [5.4 kg]."

All the clothing was made by the Inuit women, using thread made from the sinews of reindeer and narwhals.

After numerous thwarted attempts, on April 6, 1909, Peary and Henson, accompanied by four Inuit, became the first explorers to reach the North Pole.

Henson's contributions went largely unrecognized by the white public—and by Peary himself. In later years Henson finally won some of the honors he deserved. In 1937 he became the first African-American member of the Explorers Club, and in 1944 Congress awarded him a medal for co-discovering the North Pole.

WET-WEATHER Gear

WHAT DOES THE WELL-DRESSED Inuit wear to stay cozy and dry in wet weather? A raincoat made of walrus intestines. Inuit knew how to dress for the cold. In their animal-skin garments they could stay outside for hours in minus 50 degree Fahrenheit (-45.5°C) weather, in garments weighing only seven to ten pounds (3.2–4.5 kg).

Inuit wore snow goggles of wood or ivory to reduce the glare of the sun. Snow blindness—painful inflammation of the retina—was a real hazard.

Sealskin fur mittens often had two thumbs. They could be swiveled around when the palms got wet.

TRIANGLE SHIRTWAIST FIRE

FASHION DISASTER

New York City, New York, 1911

Workers, mostly young women, toiled elbow to elbow, twelve to seventeen hours a day, six days a week. Tragically, when the fire swept through the top three floors of the building, it was five minutes before the end of the workday.

The increased demand for ready-made clothing created some deplorable conditions for textile workers. In 1860 workers at the Pemberton Mills in Lawrence, Massachusetts, suffered a devastating catastrophe when shoddy construction beams collapsed and then ignited, killing or badly injuring hundreds of mill workers, most of whom were young women and girls.

Around the turn of the 20th century, many workers were laboring 12 to 17 hours a day in poorly ventilated "sweatshops." The International Ladies' Garment Workers' Union (ILGWU) joined with other progressive organizations to try to pass laws for better working conditions. Workers went on strike for increased pay, shorter hours, and an end to child labor. But many strikers were replaced by new waves of immigrant workers, desperate to eke out a living.

On March 25, 1911, a Saturday, a fire roared through the eighth floor of the Triangle Shirtwaist Company factory in New York City. It quickly spread to the ninth and tenth floors. The workers, most of them young girls from Russia and Italy, rushed to escape the flames, only to find the doors to their workrooms locked. Some made it to the one fire escape, but it collapsed, killing those on it. The fire department's ladders only reached the sixth floor. Many girls leapt to their deaths. In all, 146 people were killed. Some were as young as 12 years old.

The tragic fire called attention to the wretched working conditions of many immigrant textile workers. More details came to light. The shirtwaist workers had been working for long hours, six days a week. The owners of the factory, worried about their employees stealing from them, had routinely locked the doors to the stairwells so that they could inspect handbags as people left. After the fire, there was a public outcry for improvements in labor laws.

The factory owners were later acquitted of any wrongdoing, but the fire prompted the creation of better fire safety codes in the United States.

IT'S A TAILORED, high-necked blouse with a tight waist and puffy sleeves. Shirtwaists became fashionable around the turn of the 20th century. A craze for shirtwaists swept the country, and workers raced to fulfill the demand.

WHAT Now?

MISERABLE CONDITIONS. In April 2013 a building in Bangladesh containing several clothing factories collapsed, killing hundreds of workers. Prior to the collapse, inspection teams had deemed the building unsafe. The factory supplied garments for import by many European and American clothing companies. Government officials were blamed, but labor rights activists asserted that the real power to reform the miserable working conditions lay with the huge Western clothing companies, who put pressure on the factory owners to produce clothing more and more cheaply. Today Bangladesh has the lowest labor costs in the world.

Garment workers are poorly paid in most countries, but today, an American garment worker makes 4 times as much as a Chinese worker, 11 times what a Dominican worker makes, and 38 times more than a worker in Bangladesh.

Women garment workers make shirt collars, early 20th century

READY-TO-WEAR

ALL THE RAGE

United States, early 1900s

With the invention of the home sewing machine and the emergence of cheaper, factory-made apparel, mass-produced clothing in standardized sizes became widely available to more and more people. Improved railway transportation meant that mail-order catalogs could bring mass-produced clothing to people across the country.

Cheap rail travel brought middle- and working-class people to the seaside. The wealthy became concerned about public decency. And consider this: Prior to 1930, bathing suits were mostly made of wool.

1897

SUITABLE
Swimsuits

England, United States, 1800 – late 1900s

By the late 1800s, as the rich bought new villas by the sea, cheap railway travel made visits to the seaside easier for middle- and working-class people. Swimming grew in popularity.

The first bathing-wear was a long-sleeved, loose-fitting shift high to the neck, often made of flannel. Men's suits consisted of one-piece, woolen or serge suits, extending from the neck down to the knee.

Women swam for exercise and wore dresses to the knee and pantaloons, with heavy woolen tights underneath, and lace up shoes. It's hard to imagine just how heavy such a get-up would become when soaking wet.

Victorian bathing remained strictly segregated by gender. Women arrived at the beach fully clothed, then entered a "bathing machine," which was a hut on wheels, pulled by a donkey, and changed inside. The machine would then be dragged into the ocean, where the woman could descend into the water, out of sight of the shoreline, to swim. Often weights were sewn into the hem of her skirt to keep it from floating upward. This did little to help a swimmer stay afloat. Eventually skirts and pantaloons shortened, and necklines lowered, and by the 1890s, women's bathing costumes consisted of a blouse with knee-length drawers. But these outfits, heavy and sodden when wet, weren't meant for swimming—they were

more for wading up to the knees in the surf. In those days, few women were taught to swim, and a bather was in real danger of being swept off her feet and drowned. Many women's bathing costumes were intended to be worn with corsets.

Even men were expected to observe strict rules when it came to swimwear. Casual male bathers were required to wear skirts from 1910 to 1940. Police trawled the beaches, on the lookout for men who weren't wearing skirts over their bathing trunks, and for women whose skirts might be too far above the knee. And these policemen were armed   with rulers.

People were still expected to cover their upper bodies well into the 1920s—it wasn't until the mid-1930s that shirtless bathing trunks became acceptable. Men's navels were covered until the early 1950s, when waistlines lowered.

Swimming costumes for women remained utterly nonfunctional until the late 1920s. When Gertrude Ederle became the first woman to swim the English Channel in 1926, the popularity of swimming for sport grew.

The first two-piece bathing suits for women appeared during the 1930s, inspired by the new fad for sun tanning. These consisted of a high-waisted skirt or bathing trunks and a halter-style or brassiere-like top. After latex started being used in clothing in 1931, the industry added stretch to the suit fabric. (Spandex, a lightweight, synthetic stretchy fiber, was invented in the late 1950s.)

The bikini appeared in 1946. Its inventor named it after a group of islands in the Pacific Ocean, where the United States tested out its first atomic bomb. The bikini didn't really catch on at first and was actually outlawed in many U.S. cities. It wasn't until the 1960s that the bikini finally became popular, and it's been the bathing suit of choice for younger women ever since.

1929

Two women change on a beach in Skreenette bathing tents. These drum-shaped tents included shoulder straps so the bather could change clothes at public beaches.

IN NEW EXCITING SHADES

CUTEX

Liquid

NAIL POLISH

ALL THE Rage

THE PRACTICE OF COLORING fingernails began as far back as 3000 B.C., in ancient China and Egypt. In China certain colors were reserved for royalty—you could be put to death for wearing certain shades. But nail polish as we know it is really an invention of the 20th century.

Thanks to advances in paint technology, a new kind of lacquer was invented during the 1920s. It hardened relatively quickly and formed a shiny coating. Some modern-day pearly colors are derived from fish scales and guanine (found in bird poop), which give them a nice sheen.

JULES LEOTARD

DRESSED TO FUNCTION

England, United States, 1800s

FOR Men

The male leotard made its debut back in 1828. A man who rode bareback on horses performed his act in his underwear because his costume hadn't come back from the cleaners. Other performers realized the advantages of performing in a tight-fitting uniform, and adopted the costume. Then in 1859 a man named Jules Leotard amazed crowds with his trapeze performances while wearing a snug-fitting bodysuit. The name "leotard" became associated with him, and that's what it was called from then on.

As the century progressed, competitive male swimmers, runners, circus performers, and boxers wore even skimpier attire: legless drawers, similar to today's male briefs—but with tights. Unfortunately for the wearer, these briefs were cut the same way in the front and the back, so they rose uncomfortably over the backside.

BOXER JACK JOHNSON

A bold bicyclist in a divided skirt

FOR Women

Aside from riding (see Kicking the Habit, page 129), walking, playing croquet, and picnicking, women didn't have much chance to participate in outdoor athletic pursuits until the latter half of the 19th century (see Bloomers, page 135).

In the 1880s the Rational Dress Society was formed in England. Its goal was to promote a healthier style of dress for women that allowed some freedom of movement. Viscountess Haberton proposed that a divided skirt would be a great idea for women interested in participating in sports like tennis and yachting, but the public considered her ideas outrageous.

But in the 1890s a bicycle craze hit both America and Britain. If you've ever tried to pedal a bicycle wearing several floor-length woolen petticoats, you'll understand the problem. Skirts got caught in the gearing and had to be cut away, and a number of riders sustained serious mishaps. Knickerbockers or bloomers became the only safe garment to wear.

As the century progressed, more and more women took up ice-skating, mountaineering, swimming, golf, and tennis.

In 1934 women wore shorts for the first time to play tennis at Wimbledon.

EILEEN BENNETT WHITTINGSTALL

The demand for birds as well as other exotic animals led some species to the brink of extinction.

Plume
FAD

FASHION DISASTER

From the mid-19th century, for several decades women's hats became a major fashion focus. Even poor women wouldn't leave home without one.

By the turn of the 20th century fashionable women wore hats that were huge and elaborate, often decorated with fake fruit and flowers and feathers. The demand for feathers evolved into hats that featured a whole, stuffed bird. Millions of birds were killed for fashion, and many species nearly went extinct.

In 1889, a group of English women formed the Fur, Fin and Feather Group to try to combat the killing of animals for fashion's sake. In the United States, a similar group to protect birds, the Audubon Society, was formed in 1896. By the early 1920s federal laws were passed in both countries, banning the killing of birds for hats.

The demand for exotic animal skins led some animal species to the brink of extinction. Tortoise, alligator, shark, crocodile, snake, pig, ostrich, lizard, goat, frog, and deer have all been used—legally or illegally—for belts, shoes, purses, and jackets.

Sperm whales were driven to near extinction in the 19th century. Their oil was used for heating, oil lamps, lubricating machinery, and soap. The springy, bone-like baleen in their upper jaw was used to make corsets. And ambergris—an oily, waxy substance coughed up by sperm whales—was used as a fixative for perfume. Fortunately, kerosene was invented in 1846, which supplied a new and cheaper source of fuel oil.

For centuries, certain animal products were added to perfume to increase its lasting quality and keep its scent from evaporating too quickly. These included civet, derived from the butt of the African civet cat; castoreum, derived from beaver's butts; musk, derived from a secretion of musk deer; and ambergris. Most of these animal-derived substances smelled disgusting in their raw state (sailors on whaling ships were said to have vomited after smelling ambergris, which is saying something on a whaling ship). But when diluted and mixed they added a depth to a scent.

Because of the serious ethical issues raised in the use of these animal-derived ingredients (and, for the manufacturers, the resulting high costs) they have been replaced by synthetic versions in modern perfumes.

For as long as humans have worn clothes in cool climates, they have worn animal furs. But in modern societies, wearing furs became a status symbol. Nowadays, with central heating and mass produced, alternate types of warm outerwear, furs are no longer a necessity, but a luxury. Animals are raised on fur farms exclusively for their fur. Others are trapped and killed in the wild. Animal rights organizations have formed to combat the inhumane treatment of animals used for human consumption (as well as the use of animals for testing and experimentation in the cosmetics industry).

But the demand for furs by fashion designers—and by the consumers who want furs—persists.

WHAT Now?

MANY PEOPLE OBJECT to fur wearing as cruel to animals, but down-filled coats—a common alternative—can be just as problematic. Down is the layer of very soft feathers from the breasts of geese and ducks. While most feathers are harvested from birds raised for meat (to put it bluntly, the birds are going to die anyway), many other birds are raised in factory farms and killed just to harvest their feathers. Others have feathers plucked or clipped while they are still alive. Some geese raised in captivity must endure having their down feathers plucked every six weeks or so until they are killed for meat (or foie gras).

HOBBLE SKIRTS

ALL THE RAGE

Europe, United States, 1908 – 1912

In 1910 a popular fashion designer named Paul Poirot introduced a long, slim skirt that swathed itself closely around a woman's legs all the way to the ankle. Because it was cut straight to the ankle without a vent, women had to walk with tiny, mincing steps—the way you'd walk if your shoelaces were tied together. Architects responded by designing buildings to accommodate the fashion. Widener Library at Harvard, which was completed in 1915, has steps with short risers to accommodate women in hobble skirts.

In 1912 an American firm designed "hobble skirt" cars for city trams. These cars rose only eight inches (0.2 m) above street level, allowing women to step into the tram with relative ease. By 1914 hobble skirt tramcars could be found in cities around the world.

The hobble skirt hit its most extreme form in 1911–1912. Some employers barred their female workers from wearing them for safety reasons. Newspapers recounted several injuries and deaths from women in hobble skirts. One article in the *New York Times* reported on a hobble skirt race down 43rd Street, between Fifth and Madison.

With the outbreak of war in 1914, the hobble skirt was abandoned in favor of a shorter, fuller skirt, which allowed women the freedom to walk—and to work. Many women took jobs in factories and industries while men were off at war (see Wartime Wear, page 160).

Le Supplice d'une Ent Impossibilitt !!!

MANCHU PIGTAILS

DRESSED TO ACQUIESCE

China, 1911

The distinctive Manchu hairstyles, Hong Kong, 1905

China's Ming dynasty faltered in the 1640s, due to weak emperors and ongoing financial problems. When the army proved unable to control a peasant revolt in 1644, officials asked for help from a tribe of northern "barbarians," the Manchu (from central Manchuria). This was a mistake on the part of the Ming officials. The Manchus had grown from a small nomadic tribe of herdsmen into a militant steppe society. (See also Here Comes the Hun, page 31.) They thundered into China and established the last imperial dynasty, the Qing.

The new rulers established a new form of court dress: an upscale version of the boots, trousers, and riding coats that they had worn during their tribal days. Color played a part as well. The traditional court dress of the Ming dynasty had been red; the Qing made it yellow.

The Qing also imposed a hairstyle change. All Chinese males would be required to wear their hair in the Manchu style, which was to shave the front of the head and braid the hair at the back of the head into a long, swinging pigtail. The penalty for not wearing your hair in this fashion was death. The "queue," as it was also known, became a symbol of Qing domination over the Ming.

The Qing prohibited foot-binding, although many Chinese women ignored the edict and the practice continued (see Bound Feet, page 39). Manchu women did not bind their feet—but small feet were prized, and many Manchu women wore elevated shoes that mimicked the look of bound feet. They also tried to walk in a stiff-legged, side-to-side gait typical of women with bound feet, in an effort to achieve the look.

The Manchu ruled China until they were overthrown in 1911. The Republic of China replaced 3,000 years of imperial rule. Most men cut off their Manchu pigtails, which they perceived as symbols of the old regime.

Some Chinese who emigrated to the United States kept their queues. Ironically, the Manchu-style pigtail became a stereotype: It's how the Western media depicted a Chinese person for decades.

ZIP It!

A ZIPPER-LIKE INVENTION was first patented by Elias Howe in 1851, followed by an improved "clasp locker" in 1893. But these early versions didn't work very well and were largely ignored by the public until, after several more improvements, the modern zipper—known as the hookless fastener—was patented in 1917. Early zippers tended to rust and had to be removed from garments before washing. In the 1920s, the hookless fastener was used in rubber boots by B. F. Goodrich, and named the zipper because of the noise it made.

157

The current global trend toward mass production of clothing has diminished cultural identity for many people around the world. For the most part, everyone wears similar clothes.

10,000 B.C. - A.D. 1000
THE ANCIENT WORLD

1000 - 1400s
THE MIDDLE AGES

1400s - EARLY 1500s
THE AGE OF EXPLORATION

1500s - EARLY 1600s
THE RENAISSANCE

1600s - 1700s
THE AGE OF REASON

MID-1600s - EARLY 1800s
REVOLUTIONARY TIMES

CHAPTER NINE

WORLD AT WAR
The 20th Century & Beyond

CLASS DISMISSED

Motors and Voters · FUNCTIONAL FASHION · **Making It Work** · FLAPPER FLUSTER · **Bronzed and Beautiful** · WARTIME WEAR · **Hemline Ups and Downs** · FASCINATING FASTENERS · **Bend and Stretch** · SPACING OUT · **Fashion Don'ts** · LOW PRICE, HIGH COST · **Forecasting the Future**

MID-1700s - EARLY 1900s
MARCHING TOWARD MODERNITY

MID-1800s - EARLY 1900s
THE INDUSTRIAL REVOLUTION

THE 20TH CENTURY & BEYOND
WORLD AT WAR

WAR TIME
WEAR

With men away at war, women were employed in factories and industries. For the first time, younger women of all classes had money to spend on clothes.

FOR EVERY FIGHTER
A WOMAN WORKER
Y.W.C.A.

BACK OUR SECOND LINE OF DEFENSE
UNITED WAR WORK CAMPAIGN

World War I began in 1914 and lasted until 1918. (The United States entered the war in 1917.) When the war struck, big social changes happened quickly. In Europe and the U.S., women from all classes became involved in the war effort.

Women were recruited to work in factories and hospitals, replacing absent men in trade and industry. Because so many men enlisted, women took up jobs that had traditionally been held by those men. As a result, the upper classes found themselves without enough servants to perform tasks they'd been accustomed to leaving to others. These tasks included getting themselves dressed and coiffed. Society women gave up fussy, ornate fashions for simpler styles.

Many women cut their hair short to do war work in the factories. In England women took jobs in munitions factories, as trash collectors, tram conductors, postal workers, and railway workers. In the

United States women were recruited to serve in the U.S. Navy and Marine Corps, and were hired to serve as telephone operators, bus drivers, railway porters, miners, and workers in mills and factories. "Land girls" worked in agriculture. And many of them wore pants.

Women proved their ability to perform tasks long thought beyond women's capabilities.

Costume reflected the new role for women. For the first time in history, women's hemlines rose above the ankle.

In 1918 British women—at least those over 30—were given the right to vote. In August 1920 the 19th Amendment was passed, granting American women the right to vote.

MOTOR Trends

AS THE SPORT OF MOTORING became popular, so too did motoring fashions. The earliest cars were open, offering riders no protection from the weather or the unpaved, dusty roads. Caps, goggles, and dustcoats became essential accessories—along with high-buttoned boots in case your car broke down and you had to walk on muddy roads. Some driving gloves came with reflectors, because blinkers didn't yet exist—you had to indicate that you were turning left or right with hand signals. Women's huge hats had to be tied down with scarves and faces protected with dust-proof veils. The new Model T's could reach speeds of up to 15 miles an hour (24 km/h).

THE Flapper

ALL THE RAGE

United States, 1920s

Over the decade of the 1920s, one shocking fashion trend unrolled after another. Women cut off their long hair and wore it in a short bob, also known as the Eton crop. The huge, floppy hats that had been popular at the turn of the century were impractical for riding in the new automobiles, so women took to wearing close-fitting cloche hats. By 1926 the modern new woman was called a flapper. The name may have originated in England, when young women took to wearing galoshes (boots) left open to flap when they walked. (Other explanations of the word's origin likened young women to silvery fish that flapped around and were hard to catch hold of.)

More and more households now owned automobiles, telephones, and radios, as well as many newfangled appliances that made housework easier. Suddenly women could spend more time away from home. Some went driving. Some went dancing. And when movie stars wore

SINGER BESSIE SMITH

makeup on the big screen, every girl wanted to look like them.

The flapper enjoyed a newfound status and scandalized polite society. Not only could she now vote, she also danced to jazz, smoked cigarettes, and rode around in cars. She cast away her corset and raised her hemline. Some brazen young women rolled their stockings below the knee, revealing shocking glimpses of bare shins and kneecaps. And they wore visible makeup.

States tried to pass laws against this indecent mode of dress. A bill was introduced in Utah imposing a fine and prison time on women who wore skirts higher than three inches (7.6 cm) above the ankle. A bill in Virginia would have forbidden a woman from wearing dresses with necklines that exposed more than three inches of her throat. But these bills failed to pass.

Contrary to popular belief, not all women wore short dresses in the '20s. Hemlines rose and fell from year to year during the

decade, but dress and coat lengths hovered at calf-length. Still, in 1926, for the first time in history, some women began wearing skirts that only reached the knee.

Makeup became acceptable, even in "proper" social circles. When in 1927 a fashion designer named Coco Chanel came back from her Riviera vacation with a deep tan, sunbathing was suddenly all the rage (see Suitable Swimsuits, page 149).

Suntan lotion was invented in 1927. It was the opposite of modern-day sunblock; the idea was to attract the sun's rays.

WHAT Now?

TANNING BEDS. One hundred years ago, untanned skin was a sign that you were a person of leisure who didn't work outdoors. Women avoided the sun with parasols, hats, and veils. But in the early 1920s sun-bronzed skin became fashionable because it indicated you were free of working indoors, such as in an office or a factory.

Nowadays many people try to achieve the bronzed look more quickly by visiting tanning salons. Scientists have warned against exposure to the harmful UV rays, which can be 10 to 15 times higher in a tanning bed than from the midday sun. It can cause skin to age prematurely and, worse, to develop deadly skin cancers, including basal cell carcinoma, squamous cell carcinoma, and, the most serious, malignant melanoma.

THE Jewel IN THE CROWN

Europe, United States, 1929 – 1939

The general prosperity of the Roaring Twenties came to a screeching halt on October 21, 1929, when the stock market crashed. Banks failed and factories closed, and the grim years of the Great Depression began.

Costume jewelry—decorative ornamentation that is not made of expensive metals or precious stones—became the rage, probably out of financial necessity. Even if you hadn't lost most of your fortune, it became a symbol of bad taste to display your wealth through your jewels.

DO HEMLINES FOLLOW THE STOCK MARKET?

IT'S BEEN SUGGESTED that when the stock market drops, hemlines plunge. Certainly this was the case when the Great Depression hit in the early 1930s. As the market crashed and banks and factories closed, fashions turned more somber. Hemlines dropped well below the knee, and clothes darkened.

It's hard to draw firm conclusions about the correlation between hemlines and the economy, for the simple reason that it's only been recently—the past hundred years—that women's skirts have risen above ground level. We'll need more time and more data to make the determination.

FROM sheer TO ETERNITY

DRESSED TO IMPRESS

United States, 1939 – 1945

It's rare to find a woman today who says she likes wearing pantyhose. They're too hot in summer, too cold in winter, and they tend to snag at inconvenient times. But back in 1939, the invention of nylon changed many women's lives for the better.

Now that they were showing their lower legs for the first time in history, women welcomed the silklike sheerness of nylon as an alternative to itchy wool. The first nylon stockings flew out of the stores in 1940 and sold out practically overnight. Although few women could afford silk stockings, even those who could tended to switch over to nylon. The silk stocking market collapsed.

The first nylons, as they came to be called, came up to about mid-thigh and fastened at the top with garters and a belt. (One-piece pantyhose weren't invented until the 1960s.)

When the United States entered World War II, factories stopped producing nylon stockings and instead switched to making nylon tents and parachutes for the U.S. military. With leather in short supply, women's shoe soles were made with a wedge of cork or wood. Because elastic was rationed and couldn't be used to keep hats in place, women wore berets and crocheted hairnets, called snoods.

WHAT Now?

ECO-CHIC FLEECE

FOR CENTURIES people have worn wool to stay warm. But some people complain that it's itchy on the skin, and smelly when wet. And moths tend to chew holes in it.

Synthetic fleece was invented in 1979, and by the 1980s it became the new go-to material for cold weather dressing. In the 1990s the companies Patagonia and Polartec collaborated to make synthetic fleece from recycled plastic soda bottles.

Faced with a shortage of stockings, some American women took to drawing a black line down the backs of their bare legs to suggest the appearance of a stocking seam.

Women workers ca 1943.
CLOCKWISE FROM TOP: Women
work on a tail fuselage section of
a B-17 bomber in California, U.S.A.;
women welders in a British factory;
a woman works on a
Vengeance dive-bomber
in Tennessee, U.S.A.

Rosie
THE RIVETER

DRESSED TO FUNCTION

United States, 1941–1945

During the years of World War II (which the United States entered in 1941), women once again stepped into jobs traditionally held by men. Just as had happened during World War I, women became farm workers, nurses, and factory workers. A fictional woman named Rosie the Riveter became the emblem of any woman who had stepped into the role of industrial worker, a woman who picked up the slack left by men fighting overseas. And Rosie wanted to wear pants—especially as stockings were unavailable due to rationing and shortages.

Padded shoulders for women's shirts and jackets became popular during the 1940s. Shoulders assumed almost manly proportions during a time when women were assuming "manly" responsibilities.

With the outbreak of war, there were immediate shortages of many materials as factories switched over to producing products for the war effort. To save on fabric, men's suits were made without cuffs, pleats, or patch pockets. Women's hemlines shortened, and A-line skirts became the style because they used the least amount of fabric.

Because clothing was rationed, American and British governments advised women to "make do and mend." How-to articles appeared, advising how to make dresses from old curtains or replace frayed collars with shirttails.

Beehive
HAIRDOS

ALL THE RAGE

United States, 1950s

During World War II the U.S. government funded a research project on easily portable spray cans for soldiers, to enable them to kill disease-causing bugs while fighting on tropical Pacific islands. The spray can design became a key ingredient for pressurized cans of hairspray after the war.

Thanks to the liberal quantities of hairspray that were now available to women, the beehive hairdo became fashionable during the 1950s. Unfortunately, the early spray cans that dispensed the hairspray, as well as those containing spray paint and deodorant, contained ozone-eating chlorofluorocarbons—liquefied gases that mixed with the contents of the can in order to create the pressure inside. These were replaced in the mid-1980s by more environmentally-friendly hydrocarbons.

THE SUPREMES

THE RONETTES

BRIGITTE BARDOT

CLING-ONS

DRESSED TO FUNCTION

Switzerland, 1941

In 1941 a Swiss engineer named George de Mestral was walking his dog when he noticed small burrs stuck to his pant legs. When he examined these burrs under a microscope, he realized their tiny projections had little hooks on the end. Then he thought about how useful this principle could be for attaching clothing—and Velcro was born.

DRESSED TO
STRETCH

SPANDEX

1958 – 1959

Spandex, also called Lycra, is a synthetic fiber that allows clothing to stretch. The material was invented in the late 1950s by a chemist. Because it contains no rubber and resists perspiration, it revolutionized swimsuits, underwear, and disco jeans. The stretchy tape on diapers contains Spandex, as do pantyhose, bra straps, and socks. Where would superheroes be without it?

LEISURE SUITS

Polyester, a plastic-based fiber developed by British scientists during World War II, was made into washable, wrinkle-proof "leisure suits" after the war. They felt almost like cotton—except that they were stultifying in warm weather and highly flammable if the wearer was unfortunate enough to be caught in a fire.

Advertisements featured models showering in their leisure suits, swimming in them, and wearing them for days and days in a row without the need of a pressing. By the 1970s polyester suits had become a symbol of bad taste and were roundly mocked by all but those who wore them.

Polyester clothing is making a comeback. Some people love it simply for the fact that you can drop an entire spaghetti dinner down your front and wipe it away with little evidence that it was ever there. And shirts that contain a blend of polyester and cotton have liberated many a harried person from needing to iron a shirt before work.

Today polyester is the most popular man-made fiber, accounting for more than 40 percent of all fibers produced today. When it is blended into wool, silk, or cotton, it brings down the price of the garment, although many would say it also lessens the garment's quality.

In the days when more people knew how to sew, people paid closer attention to the quality of the fabric they were buying. The better the quality of the cloth, the longer the clothing was likely to last—and if you'd made it yourself, you'd want it to last.

Next time you are considering buying a new article of clothing, check the label. Is it a natural fiber, like cotton, wool, linen, or silk? Or an artificial fiber? Or is it a blend?

Because of its molecular structure—strong but elastic—polyester can spring back into shape after wear and look just as awful as when new.

THE **G**REAT LEVELER

Europe, United States, 1950s

In the past rags and filth had been the most reliable way to tell who was very poor. In the 19th century cleanliness marked the difference between rich and poor. In the days before running water, only the rich could afford regular baths, with water lugged in, heated, and lugged out again by servants. In the 20th century, for the first time in history, poor people could not be so readily identified by their clothes. Improved plumbing meant most people could bathe, and mass production of clothing meant inexpensive clothes were within reach of people at nearly every income level. The only visible difference between a working-class man and an upper-class gentleman would be the quality of the cloth of his suit, and the way it was cut.

No sooner did couture designers show new collections but cheaper clothing manufacturers knocked off the designs at prices that were affordable to those on a budget. Or women sewed versions of the designs themselves. Poverty did not, of course, cease to exist, but the visual reminder of it did.

Post-war affluence in 1950s America brought the latest fashions within reach of more and more middle-class people. But it was a time of deep prejudice. The higher standard of living remained out of reach for most people of color.

THE MINI-SKIRT

ALL THE RAGE

1960s

The most striking fashion trend of the 1960s was the miniskirt. Never before had women exposed so much of their legs. Although touted as the ultimate in freedom of movement for women, the tight, tiny skirts made getting in and out of cars a challenge, not to mention picking up a dropped pencil.

The sixties were a time of great upheaval. Women were increasingly battling discrimination and demanding equal pay for equal work. Just as had happened in the days of the hobble skirt, women's fashion grew more restrictive just as they were fighting for more freedom.

SPACE-AGE FASHION

1960s – 1970s

WACKY FASHIONS

1970s – 1980s

When the first astronauts walked on the moon in 1969, the "space age" look became popular.

Advancements in technology in the latter part of the 20th century paved the way for outrageous fashions that people from previous centuries probably couldn't have imagined.

Notable mostly for the strides toward equality and social justice made by women and African Americans, the 1970s and '80s may also be remembered for their unique fashions. Hair parted in the center, platform shoes, disco wear, and, in the '80s, huge shoulder pads and power suits for women may look hilarious to us now, but even some of these more dubious fashions have enjoyed a renaissance, of sorts, recently.

SINGER GRACE JONES

Cheap clothing comes at a high cost—
it damages the environment, hurts the
economy, and, at times, leads to a lot of
human misery in developing countries.

WHY DO WE Wear THAT?

Modern Day

In the United States we produce about 2 percent of the clothing that American consumers buy. The rest is imported from other countries. Today what's available falls into two categories: high-end, designer clothing that is far out of reach of most people, and inexpensive, more cheaply made, mass-produced clothing, which is what most of us wear. Nowadays we toss away clothes we've barely worn in favor of the newest, latest trend, because we can—clothing is no longer such a large percentage of a household's budget. We pay less today for clothes (as a share of our income) than we ever have in history. Where families once mended, altered, and refashioned clothing, we now discard it and buy something else. But cheap clothing comes at a high cost to the environment, the economy, and human suffering.

Forty-one percent of the clothes we wear are made in China. Much of the rest is made in countries where the garment industry is badly regulated. Poor safety standards and low wages make for miserable labor conditions.

WHAT CAN YOU DO?

See how much more interesting your history book will be now that you know more about the history of what people wore?

And your knowing that history may affect what kind of clothes you

Be aware of what you wear. Look at the tag on your T-shirt. Find out where it was made. Then do a little research into store brands that partner with manufacturers that give their workers a decent wage and standard of living. It may be worth it to pay a few more dollars for clothing made by conscientious

manufacturers.

Now that you've read this book, you may never look at portraits and photos from the past the same way again. Going to museums will be a lot more fun.

When you see a woman in a farthingale, you'll know she probably has no underwear on. Or that the Founding Father signing the Declaration of Independence is wearing formal britches so tight he can't sit down in them. You'll know that the hats worn by Pilgrims were made of beaver pelts; the red coats of British soldiers were dyed with ground-up cochineal insects; the purple stripes of Roman emperors' togas were dyed with rotten snails. And you'll appreciate the untold number of people who toiled to make these clothes—those who soaked and scraped and boiled and stitched and starched and pinned.

choose to wear. Maybe you'll check the labels on clothes before you buy them—because now you know something about the history of cotton, wool, linen, and silk, and also the history of artificial fibers, and of dyeing clothes different colors.

The world has changed. Fashions have evolved. Clothes are cheaper than ever, but the hidden costs in human misery, pollution, and waste have risen. Technology has created new production techniques and body-altering procedures that people in the past would not have dreamed possible. But has our desire to create an image of ourselves through our clothing really changed all that much?

Just as people did in the past, many people today—especially those who are in the public eye—make some pretty wacky choices in their effort to reshape and redefine themselves. Think liposuction, face-lifts, tanning salons, contaminants in cosmetics,

implants, tattoos, thongs, stiletto heels, hair plugs, platform shoes, body piercings, lip augmentation, and Botox. In light of the choices people make in our day and age, do corsets, crinolines, codpieces,

pattens, and powdered wigs seem all that outrageous?

Fashion gives us a visual reference point for every moment in history. And having looked behind us at where we came from, perhaps we'll be able to look around us with a deeper understanding of who we are today.

And what about the future? No one has ever been able to predict with much accuracy what the next fashion trends are going to be. But in recent decades, fashion trends seem to have shifted from top down to bottom up. Street styles, hip-hop artists, and athletes have started new trends that are then copied by high-fashion designers. Think about that. The fact that "street fashion" can set trends is a very modern notion. As late as the last century, the laboring classes had no fashion trends, to speak of. People wore rags, or one set of clothes. They couldn't afford to upgrade, update, or refashion their look. Cheap production of clothing has caused that to change.

Clothes are cheaper than they've ever been—in that sense history has changed a great deal. But haute couture is just as far out of the reach of the middle-class working person as it was in the 16th century. In that sense history hasn't changed much at all.

Still, new inventions are emerging. Soon you may be wearing electric clothes that can harness your body heat and power your smartphone. Athletes will be wearing analytical underwear that can analyze how hard they're exercising their hamstrings and glutes. New eco-friendly fabric dyeing techniques are being developed that use heat transfer, which saves gallons of water, uses much less energy, and produces fewer harmful by-products.

Soon you may be wearing mood sweaters that reveal your emotions as they change color, shoes that act as mini vacuum cleaners, socks with sensors in them that can prevent running injuries, and eyeglasses that respond to voice commands and display information right on the lenses. In fact, these new innovations exist already.

How will the reflection of our society look to future generations? What will your grandchildren laugh at? What will they view with horror? It may be fake tans, low-slung jeans, tattoos, yoga pants, dip-dyed hair, or snapback hats worn backward.

YOU'LL HAVE SOME EXPLAINING TO DO!

Here's a fashion time line of human history. In order to fit everything on these two pages, we condensed a few centuries, expanded others, and then folded it up a bit. Fashion events appear on the top; major historical events appear on the bottom.

10,000 Neolithic era: Loom is invented; first spinning and weaving of yarn

5000 First linen in Egypt; first leather tanners in Mesopotamia

3500 First cotton grown in Peru

2600 Silk is discovered in China

Egyptian Middle Kingdom **2100 – 1784**

Bull jumping in Minoa **2000 – 1500**

1100 First known armor in China, made from rhinoceros hides

Assyrians sweep across western Asia **884**

800 Phoenicians produce Tyrian purple dye from rotten shells

First Olympic Games **776**

500s First trousers worn by Persians

Emergence of the Celts **500**

500 Persian soldiers use hot tongs to curl their beards for battle

Golden Age of Greece begins **480**

Foundation of the Han dynasty in China **207**

Rome defeats Carthage and becomes **201** the major Mediterranean power

Silk Road opens **126**

Emergence of the Roman Empire **27**

B.C. A.D.

43 Rome invades Britain

410 Visigoths sack Rome

452 Attila invades Rome

527 Justinian becomes emperor of Byzantium

Secret of silk stolen from **552** China and brought to Byzantium

The glass mirror is invented **636**

662 Birth of Islam

787 First Viking raids in Britain

300 – 900 Maya classic period

Foot-binding practice **1000** begins in China

1096 First Crusade

The first gloves in Europe appear **1175**

1200 – 1500 Aztec civilization in Mexico

1231 Mongol conquest of northern China and Korea

1348 First appearance of the Black Death in Europe and Egypt

1492 Columbus "discovers" the New World

1501 First African slaves shipped to Hispaniola

1519 Cortés meets Moctezuma

1534 King Henry VIII splits from the Catholic Church

1558 Elizabeth I assumes the throne of England

1607 Settlement of the Jamestown colony in Virginia

1620 Voyage of the *Mayflower*

Louis XIV revokes the Edict **1685** of Nantes; the Huguenots flee persecution

Peter the Great assumes **1689** the throne of Russia

1649 Charles I executed; Oliver Cromwell establishes the Commonwealth of England

Louis XIV assumes the throne in France; starts a trend for men in high heels
1661

182

Latex, invented in the '20s, **1931** first used in fabrics

1934 First time a woman wears shorts at Wimbledon

1939 Nylon is invented

1940s Acrylic (invented in the '30s) first used in fabrics; it is made from a petrochemical that approximates wool

1929 Wall Street crash, beginning of Great Depression

1920 American women achieve universal suffrage— the right to vote

World War II **1939 – 1945**

1946 First bikini is modeled

1914 – 1918 World War I

India and Pakistan establish independent **1947** states free of British rule

1948 Invention of Velcro; becomes common 1955

Zip fastener (zipper) **1913** is invented

1911 Triangle Shirtwaist Fire

1911 End of Manchu dynasty in China

1953 Polyester (invented in 1940s), a plastic-based fiber, becomes popular

1959 Spandex (Lycra) is invented by a chemist

Rayon is invented, made **1910** from chemically treated wood pulp; it imitates silk but is not as durable

Neil Armstrong becomes first **1969** person on the moon

1983 Polarfleece (polybenzimidazole fiber) is made from recycled plastic soda bottles

1908 Model T Ford

Audubon Society is formed **1896**

1890s Bicycle craze

Ebenezer Butterick produces **1863** the first home sewing patterns in different sizes

1861 American Civil War begins

William Perkin creates the **1856** first synthetic dyes

Levi Strauss invents first blue jeans **1853**

1700 For the first time, a cape is used in bullfighting

Amelia Bloomer steps out in her **1851** shocking new costume

Isaac Singer refines and patents the **1851** sewing machine

1700s Pockets are introduced; before then, belongings were carried in a pouch

Bathing costumes become popular **1850s**

1715 Folding umbrellas appear in Paris

Charles Goodyear invents **1839** vulcanized rubber, paving the way for rubber-soled shoes and waterproof galoshes

1732 Britain passes the Hat Act, angering American colonists

1733 The flying shuttle loom is invented

1837 Queen Victoria assumes the throne of England

Signing of the Declaration **1776** of Independence

The British surrender at Yorktown **1781** (American Revolution)

1825 Britain's first passenger railways begin

Start of the French Revolution **1789**

1793 Eli Whitney invents the cotton gin

1796 Jenner discovers smallpox vaccine; patches soon go out of fashion

Charles Macintosh **1823** creates a rainproof coat

1797 The first washing machine is patented

Luddites wreck **1811** machinery in England

1818 Britain establishes rule over India

Napoleon becomes emperor **1804**

As a kid I generally enjoyed field trips to museums, as long as there was interesting stuff to see like medieval armor, dinosaur bones, or pictures of people wearing weird stuff. But I was often frustrated by the exhibit descriptions that were supposed to explain these pictures—the lack of information they provided. What was going on here? That huge cartwheel collar—how could you possibly eat soup while wearing such a thing? That hoop skirt the size of my teacher's desk—how did the wearer manage to go to the bathroom? Those skin-tight, knee-length breeches—how could you sit down without splitting them up the back? Hats shaped like three-foot (0.9-m)-long ice-cream cones, warriors in fishnet stockings, painful-looking bound feet, edible arsenic cosmetic wafers, big black face patches—just ... why? What were people thinking?

So I grew up, researched my questions, and wrote this book. I read a lot of books about events in history, and a lot of books about the history of fashion. But this isn't technically a book about the history of fashion. Such books, while fascinating to look at, tend not to give you much historical context. They don't explain why people wore what they wore, how they lived their lives, how (or whether) they did their laundry. I like to think of this book as a mash-up: the history behind what people wore, or, if you prefer, history through fashion.

Thanks to the Metropolitan Museum of Art and the American Museum of Natural History, both of which I visited on numerous occasions as I researched the book; sculptor and art historian Mark Mennin for answering my endless questions about ancient statuary; Christopher Lightfoot, curator of Greek and Roman art at the Metropolitan Museum of Art; costume historian Mimi Duphily, for teaching me about spinning, weaving, and sewing; all the librarians at The Taft School for their endless support; Nandini Bajpai for her close reading of sections about India; Cassie Willson and Caroline Blatz for research assistance (okay, Cassie's my teenage daughter and Caroline's her best friend, but they did an awesome job); my fantastic editors, Jennifer Emmett and Ariane Szu-Tu; brilliant art director Jim Hiscott; tireless and patient photo editors Lori Epstein and Hillary Leo (I would think Jim, Lori, and Hillary were ready to throttle me as we debated what images to include for this complex project, but they remained so very gracious, and hugely enthusiastic about the book); my wonderful agent, Caryn Wiseman; and the Society of Children's Book Writers and Illustrators.

And a dedication, of sorts, to all the people across the centuries who toiled away cultivating, dyeing, spinning, weaving, sewing, laundering, and assembling so many of the fashions we've seen in this book. Their names have been lost to history, but they've nevertheless profoundly shaped it.

BIBLIOGRAPHY

SOURCES QUOTED

[page 25] "Wish as you might, a Spartan girl ..." Euripides as quoted in William Harlan Hale's *Horizon Book of Ancient Greece* (New York: American Heritage, 1965), p. 263.

[page 31] "they at first thought she had lost a leg" Michael and Ariane Batterberry, *Fashion: The Mirror of History* (New York: Holt, Rinehart and Winston, 1977), p. 63.

[page 56] "fiery furnaces, boiling water ..." Amy Butler Greenfield, *A Perfect Red*, p. 244.

[page 75] "inadvertently ... eat about 4 pounds of lipstick" *Glamour* magazine, June 2002.

[page 85] "nitty coats and stinking hose" as quoted in Emily Cockayne's *Hubbub: Filth, Noise & Stench in England, 1600–1770* (New Haven: Yale University Press, 2007), p. 78.

[page 103] "for their Size, Hair, Beauty ..." *Gentleman's Magazine*, 2 March 1732, pp. 660–661.

[page 107] "I should have taken him for a pig farmer ..." Mme Vigee-Le Brun as quoted in Ronald Clark's *Benjamin Franklin: A Biography* (New York: Random House, 1983), p. 341.

[page 134] "the bustle was sitting next to you on the bench" Eline Canter Cremers-van Der Does, *The Agony of Fashion*, p. 96.

[page 138] "Society beauties whirling through waltzes ..." John Carey, review of James C. Whorton's *The Arsenic Century*, accessed January 24, 2010, timesonline.co.uk.

[page 143] "the court of the decapitated Louis XVI" Batterberry, p. 256.

[page 145] "a deerskin hooded coat" Robert E. Peary, *The Secrets of Polar Travel*, archive.org/stream/secretsofpolar-tr00pear/secretsofpolartr00pear_djvu.txt.

SELECT BIBLIOGRAPHY

All the Rage. Alexandria, VA: Time-Life, 1992.

Batterberry, Michael and Ariane. *Fashion: The Mirror of History.* New York: Holt, Rinehart and Winston, 1977.

Bryson, Bill. *At Home: A Short History of Private Life.* New York: Doubleday, 2010.

Canter Cremers-van Der Does, Eline. *The Agony of Fashion.* Poole, [Eng.] UK: Blandford, 1980.

Cline, Elizabeth L. *Overdressed: The Shockingly High Cost of Cheap Fashion.* New York: Portfolio/Penguin, 2012.

Cunnington, Phillis. *Costume of Household Servants, From the Middle Ages to 1900.* London: A. and C. Black, 1974.

Cunnington, Phillis, and Anne Buck. *Children's Costume in England. From the Fourteenth to the End of the Nineteenth Century.* London: A. & C. Black, 1965.

Davidson, Michael Worth, and Neal V. Martin, eds. *Reader's Digest Everyday Life Through the Ages.* London: Reader's Digest Association, 1992.

Douglass, Frederick. *Narrative of the Life of Frederick Douglass: An American Slave.* Edited by William L. Andrews and William S. McFeely. New York: W. W. Norton, 1997.

Ewing, Elizabeth. *Dress and Undress: A History of Women's Underwear.* New York: Drama Book Specialists, 1978.

Flanders, Judith. *Inside the Victorian Home: A Portrait of Domestic Life in Victorian England.* New York: W. W. Norton, 2004.

Greenfield, Amy Butler. *A Perfect Red: Empire, Espionage, and the Quest for the Color of Desire.* New York: HarperCollins, 2005.

Madden, Thomas F. *Venice: A New History.* New York: Viking, 2012.

Panati, Charles. *Panati's Extraordinary Endings of Practically Everything and Everybody.* New York: Perennial Library, 1987.

Pendergast, Sara, Tom Pendergast, and Sarah Hermsen. *Fashion, Costume, and Culture: Clothing, Headwear, Body Decorations, and Footwear Through the Ages.* Detroit: UXL, 2004.

Picard, Liza. *Dr Johnson's London: Coffee Houses and Climbing Boys, Medicine, Toothpaste and Gin, Poverty and Press-Gangs, Freakshows and Female Education.* New York: St. Martin's, 2001.

Picard, Liza. *Elizabeth's London: Everyday Life in Elizabethan London.* New York: St. Martin's, 2003.

Picard, Liza. *Victorian London: The Tale of a City, 1840–1870.* New York: St. Martin's, 2005.

Robinson, Tony. *The Worst Jobs in History: Two Thousand Years of Miserable Employment.* London: Pan, 2007.

Steele, Valerie. *The Corset: A Cultural History.* New Haven: Yale University Press, 2001.

Ward, Susan. "Swimwear." In *Encyclopedia of Clothing and Fashion*, edited by Valerie Steele. Farmington Hills, MI: Charles Scribner's Sons, 2005. pp. 250–255.

Waugh, Norah. *Corsets and Crinolines.* New York: Theatre Arts, 1970.

BOOKS FOR YOUNGER READERS

You Wouldn't Want to . . . series (Scholastic)

This multibook series examines the darker side of everyday life in the past with humor and kid-friendly illustrations, captions, and sidebars.

The Greenwood Press *Daily Life Through History* Series

A multibook series for older kids that provides an in-depth exploration of daily life throughout history. Narrative chapters include photos, maps, and other ready reference materials.

If You Lived . . . series (Scholastic)

For younger readers, these books are written in an accessible question-and-answer format.

Freedman, Russell. *Kids at Work: Lewis Hine and the Crusade Against Child Labor.* Boston: HMH Books for Young Readers, 1998.

Marrin, Albert. *Flesh and Blood So Cheap: The Triangle Fire and Its Legacy.* New York: Knopf Books for Young Readers, 2011.

ONLINE RESOURCES AND PLACES TO VISIT IN PERSON

The Museum at the Fashion Institute of Technology

227 W. 27th St.
New York, New York 10001
www.fitnyc.edu/museum.asp

Includes temporary exhibits featuring histories of various fashion trends. See the exhibition schedule online.

Works of Lewis Hine at the Museum of Modern Art

11 W. 53rd St.
New York, New York 10019
www.moma.org/collection/artist
.php?artist_id=2657

Lewis Hine Collection at the Library of Congress

101 Independence Ave., SE
Washington, DC 20540
www.loc.gov/pictures/collection/nclc

An online exhibit of 5,100 photographs by Lewis Hine, documenting working and living conditions of children in the United States between 1908 and 1924.

Gallery of Costume at the Kent State University Museum

515 Hilltop Dr.
Kent, OH 44242
www2.kent.edu/museum/index.cfm

The museum provides a close look at historic and contemporary fashion and costumes from the 17th to 21st centuries.

The Costume Institute at the Metropolitan Museum of Art

1000 5th Ave.
New York, New York 10028
www.metmuseum.org/about-the-museum/
museum-departments/curatorial-departments/
the-costume-institute

Includes over 35,000 costumes and accessories. The museum features at least one special exhibition every year highlighting significant cultural trend in fashion history.

The Worth and Mainbocher Online Haute Couture Exhibit

collections.mcny.org/C.aspx?
VP3=CMS3&VF=MNYO28_4

Part of the Museum of the City of New York's online offerings.

Bata Shoe Museum Online Exhibit

www.allaboutshoes.ca/en

The Bata Shoe Museum of Toronto, Ontario, features an online exhibition called "All About Shoes" that showcases footwear throughout human history.

"The First Ladies" Exhibition at the National Museum of American History

1000 Jefferson Dr., SW
Washington, DC 20004
americanhistory.si.edu/exhibitions/first-ladies

"The First Ladies" exhibition at the Smithsonian and online features gowns from the First Ladies Collection.

National Museum of African American History and Culture

As of this writing, this Smithsonian museum is set to open in 2015 on the National Mall in Washington, D.C.

There are a number of other museums around the country dedicated to African-American history and culture, including the following:

Charles H. Wright Museum of African American History

Detroit, MI
thewright.org

DuSable Museum of African American History

Chicago, IL
www.dusablemuseum.org

Rock and Roll Hall of Fame

1100 E. 9th St.
Cleveland, OH 44114
rockhall.com/exhibits

The Rock and Roll Hall of Fame contains the iconic clothes and costumes worn by music legends such as the Beatles, Elvis, and Michael Jackson.

The Hat Museum

1928 S.E. Ladd Ave.
Portland, OR 97214
www.thehatmuseum.com

The Hat Museum features a collection of hats in a variety of styles from past eras.

Plimoth Plantation

137 Warren Ave.
Plymouth, MA 02360
www.plimoth.org/

Plimoth Plantation is an authentic recreation of the original settlement of the Plymouth Colony in the 17th century, and includes a Wampanoag living history exhibit.

Colonial Williamsburg

Williamsburg, VA 23187
www.colonialwilliamsburg.com

A place where kids can experience firsthand what life was like in colonial America during revolutionary times.

The Wisconsin Historical Museum Online Children's Clothing Collection

30 N. Carroll St.
Madison, WI 53703
museumcollections.wisconsinhistory.org/picts-rch.cfm?ParentID=376566

A place to browse through over 2,000 articles of children's clothing online by decade, gender, or type.

INDEX

ART = Art Resource, NY; BAL = The Bridgeman Art Library; GET = Getty Images; SS = Shutterstock; TGC = The Granger Collection, NYC

FRONT COVER (runway), Blend Images/Alamy; (man in red) Portrait of a man in red by Flemish School, The Royal Collection/BAL; (woman in purple) The Print Collector/Heritage-Images/GET; (man in white), BAL/GET; cover (woman in blue) TGC; (samurai) Ira Block/National Geographic Creative; **BACK COVER** (French revolution woman), Apic/GET; (armor), Suit of armour with poulaines, Musee de l'Armee, Paris, France/BAL; (Native American king), Etow Oh Koam, King of the River Nations by Verelst, Johannes or Jan/BAL; (futuristic dress), 2/Ocean/Corbis; (colorful feet), The Print Collector/GET; **FRONT FLAP** (fig leaf), Scisetti Alfio/SS; **BACK FLAP** (up), Bruno Ratensperger; (lo), Scott McDermott; **CASE COVER** (front), Susanna Fieramosca Naranjo/E+/GET; (back), Siede Preis/Photographer's Choice RF/GET; **REPEATING ICONS:** (ch 1 icon), Head of the child king Tutankhamun, New Kingdom, Egyptian National Museum/BAL; (ch 2 icon), Suit of armour with poulaines, by French School; Musee de l'Armee/BAL; (ch 3 icon), Etow Oh Koam, King of the River Nations by Verelst, Johannes or Jan/BAL; (ch 4 icon), Portrait of Queen Elizabeth of Bohemia by Peake, Robert, the Elder/BAL; (ch 5 icon), Madame de Ventadour with Louis XIV and his heirs, Wallace Collection, London, UK/BAL; (ch 6 icon), Apic/GET; (ch 7 icon), Romualdo Alinari's children, Adele and Arturo, on stilts, Florence, c.1875 by Fratelli Alinari/BAL; (ch 8 icon), Harold M. Lambert/Lambert/GET; (ch 9 icon), 2/Ocean/Corbis; (fig leaf) Scisetti Alfio/SS

FRONT OF BOOK: 1, Igor Kovalchuk/iStockphoto; 2, The Print Collector/GET; 3 (UPLE), Ivy Close Images/Alamy; 3 (UPRT), Ivy Close Images/Alamy; 3 (CTR), Romualdo Alinari's children, Adele and Arturo, on stilts, Florence, c.1875, by Fratelli Alinari/BAL; 3 (LOLE), Harold M. Lambert/Lambert/GET; 3 (LORT), 2/Ocean/Corbis; 4, Keystone-France/Gamma-Keystone/GET; 5, A detail of a frieze on the south wall of the Hall of Pillars in the tomb of vizier Ramose/BAL; 5, Detail of one of the suits of Samurai armour displayed in the Green Room; Snowshill Manor, Gloucestershire, UK, National Trust Photographic Library/Andreas von Einsiedel/BAL; 5, Portrait of Queen Elizabeth I - The Armada Portrait by Gower, George/BAL; 5, Architectural Fantasy by Joli, Antonio/RAI; 6, Christie's Images Ltd/Corbis; 6 (UPRT), Three women with a bicycle, England, by English Photographer/RAI; 6 (LOLE), Everett Collection Inc/Alamy; 6 (LORT), Conde Nast Archive/Corbis; 7, Scisetti Alfio/SS, 8, Scisetti Alfio/SS

CHAPTER 1: 10, INTERFOTO/Alamy; 12, Cavemen during the Ice Age by Kranz, Wilhelm; Bibliotheque des Arts Decoratifs, Paris, France/BAL; 13 (UP), somchaij/SS; 13, SuperStock; 14, Ms 202 fol.10 Weaving, by Chinese school/Bibliotheque Municipale, Poitiers, France/BAL; 14, NATUREWORLD/Alamy; 15, Emperor Justinian I, Byzantine School, San Vitale, Ravenna, Italy/BAL; 15, Tarker/Corbis; 16, Tutankhamen's Tomb, De Agostini Picture Library/G. Dagli Orti/BAL; 17, Album/ART; 17, SSPL/Science Museum/GET; 17, Head of the child king Tutankhamun, Egyptian National Museum, Cairo, Egypt/BAL; 18-19, Ladies of the Minoan Court, Minoan; Archaeological Museum of Heraklion, Crete, Greece/BAL; 20, NGS Image Collection/The Art Archive at ART; 20, Dr. Collette M. Dowell/Circular Times/Moving Forward Publications; 21, Ivy Close Images/Alamy; 22, WILDLIFE GmbH/Alamy; 22, Paul Harcourt Davies/naturepl.com; 22, Adrian Davies/naturepl.com; 22, thongchai-tjn/SS; 22, motorolka/SS; 22, David Pike/Minden Pictures; 23, Thomas Holton/23 (LORT), David Acosta Allely/SS; 24, Ancient Olympic games by Lovell, Tom/BAL; 25, Two dancers in Poseidon's Temple, Sounion, Greece by Williams, Maynard Owen/BAL; 25, SuperStock; 25, TGC; 26, Hulton Archive/GET; 27, Dual Carriageway by Fraser, Olivia/BAL; 27, Procession Of Women At Gangaur Festival/Omniphoto/BAL; 27, Moviepix/GET; 28, Horace, Virgil and Varius by Jalabert, Charles Francois, Musee des Beaux-Arts, Nimes, France/BAL; 28, ART; 29, Pictish Man Holding a Shield by John White/BAL; 30, SuperStock; 30, SSPL/Science Museum/GET; 31, Attila the Hun torturing a captive by Embleton, Ron/BAL; 31, Attis dancing, Hellenistic period from Myrina by Greek, Louvre, Paris, France/BAL; 32, Universal Images Group Editorial/GET; 33, Universal Images Group Editorial/GET; 33, GET Europe/GET

CHAPTER 2: 34-35, Susanna Fieramosca Naranjo/GET; 36, ART; 36, Ms Fr 2810 fol.274 Pilgrims in front of the Church of the Holy Sepulchre by Boucicaut Master/Bibliotheque Nationale, Paris, France/BAL; 37, PRISMA ARCHIVO/Alamy; 37, Baronb/SS; 38, The Print Collector/age fotostock; 38, ART; 39, AFP/GET; 39, SuperStock; 40, Bruno Morandi/GET; 41, BAL/GET; 41, BAL/GET; 41, Bob Thomas/GET; 42, Gianni Dagli Orti/The Art Archive at ART; 43, Young Percival Questions Sir Owen by Crane, Walter, Russell-Cotes Art Gallery and Museum, Bournemouth, UK/BAL; 44, Hulton Fine Art Collection/GET; 45, Agincourt - The Impossible Victory 25 October 1415 by Embleton, Ron; Private Collection/BAL; 45, King Henry V by English School/BAL; 46, fotocociredef73/SS; 46, De Agostini/GET; 46, Hulton Archive/GET; 47, The Print Collector/Heritage-Images/GET; 47, Suit of armour with poulaines by French School, Musee de l'Armee, Paris, France/BAL; 47, iStockphoto; 48, Hulton Royals/GET; 48, The Picture Desk Ltd/ART; 49, Young elegant man in 1480, illustration from 'Costumes de Paris a travers les siecles' by H. Gourdon de Genouillac, engraved by Stablo/BAL; 49, Hulton Archive/GET; 50, Portrait of Gerolamo Savonarola by Alessandro Bonvicino/Verona, Castelvecchio/De Agostini Picture Library/A. Dagli

Orti/BAL; 50, The Work of Savonarola by McBride, Angus/BAL; 51, Werner Forman/ART; 51, The Print Collector/Heritage-Images/GET

CHAPTER 3: 52-53, TGC; 54, AZA/Archive Zabé/ART; 55, Christopher Columbus by Piombo, Sebastiano del (S. Luciani)/Metropolitan Museum of Art,/BAL; 55, iStockphoto; 56, The Encounter between Hernan Cortes and Montezuma II, from 'Le Costume Ancien ou Moderne' by Jules Ferrario/Bibliotheque des Arts Decoratifs, Paris, France/BAL; 56, Roy 15 E III f.269 Dyeing cloth, from Des Proprietes des Choses by Bartholomeus Anglicus/BAL; 57, Etow Oh Koam, King of the River Nations by Verelst, Johannes or Jan/BAL; 57, Aldo Tutino/ART; 58, Hulton Archive/GET; 59, Juan Silva/GET; 59, Fuse/GET; 59, Caiaimage/GET

CHAPTER 4: 60-61, Portrait of Marchesa Maria Serra Pallavicino by Rubens, Peter Paul, National Trust Photographic Library/Derrick E. Witty BAL; 62, Nimatallah/ART; 63, The Fall of the Roman Empire in the West by Embleton, Ron/BAL; 63, anshar/SS; 63, Lonely Planet Images/GET; 64, Courtesan Antea by Francesco Mazzola, known as Parmigianino, Naples, Museo Nazionale Di Capodimonte/BAL; 64, Cosmin Manci/SS; 65, The Tasburgh Group: Lettice Cressy, Lady Tasburgh of Bodney, Norfolk and her Children by English School/BAL; 66, The Public Punishment of Prisoners by the Court of the Inquisition in Spanish School, Mithra/Index/BAL; 67, Portrait of Queen Elizabeth I - The Drewe Portrait by Gower, George/BAL; 68, Portrait of Queen Elizabeth of Bohemia by Peake, Robert, the Elder/BAL; 69, Robert Devereux, 2nd Earl of Essex by Gheeraerts, Marcus, the Younger, Woburn Abbey, Bedfordshire, UK/BAL; 70, The Wedding Dance by Bruegel, Pieter the Elder, Detroit Institute of Arts/BAL; 71, Queen Elizabeth I knighting Francis Drake by Matania, Fortunino/RAI; 72, Landing at Jamestown, 1607 by English School/BAL; 72, Kharbine-Tapabor/ART; 72, alexsvirid/SS; 73, Portrait of a woman, possibly Frances Cotton, Lady Montagu, of Boughton Castle, Northamptonshire by Peake, Robert, the Elder, Yale Center for British Art/BAL; 74, Portrait of a Woman, previously identified as Mary Fitzalan, Duchess of Norfolk by Eworth or Ewoutsz, Hans, Yale Center for British Art/BAL; 75, Gloves presented to Queen Elizabeth I on her visit to Oxford University in 1566, Ashmolean Museum, University of Oxford/BAL; 75, Jeanne III d'Albret, Queen of Navarre by Clouet, Francois, Musee Conde, Chantilly, France/BAL; 75, Lee Hacker/Alamy; 75, Graham Oliver/Alamy

CHAPTER 5: 76-77, A Cavalier by Detti, Cesare-Auguste/Christie's Images/BAL; 78, Off Duty by Conti, Tito; Private Collection/Christie's Images/BAL; 79, A Cavalier by Detti, Cesare-Auguste/Christie's Images/BAL; 79, Portrait of Mary Villiers, Lady Herbert of Shurland by Dyck, Sir Anthony van, Timken Museum of Art, San Diego/BAL; 79, Portrait of Oliver Cromwell by Walker, Robert/BAL; 79, Portrait of a Young Woman by Palamedesz, Anthonie (Stevers)/Christie's Images/BAL, 80, ART, 81, INTERFOTO/Alamy; 82, Madame de Ventadour with Louis XIV and his heirs, Wallace Collection, London, UK/BAL; 83, Sergio Anelli/Electa/Mondadori Portfolio/GET; 84, ART; 85, The Lunch by Velazquez, Diego Rodriguez de Silva, Museum of Fine Arts, Budapest, Hungary/BAL; 85, A girl chopping onions by Dou, Gerrit or Gerard, The Royal Collection/BAL; 86, ART; 86, Museum Associates/LACMA/ART; 86, DeA Picture Library/TGC; 88, ART; 89, A Soaker or Real Cat and Dog Day, engraved by G. Hunt, published by Thomas McLean, London/BAL; 89, pukach/SS; 89, A Kitchen Scene with a Maid Drawing Water from a Well by Slingelandt, Pieter van, Johnny van Haeften Gallery, London, UK/BAL; 90, Patch-Box made by M. Phillippe/BAL; 90, NTPL/John Hammond/ART

CHAPTER 6: 92-93, French Revolution; National Convention and the Reign of Terror, Colored engraving by Piloty/BAL; 94, Museum of London/Heritage-Images/GET; 94, Hulton Fine Art Collection/GET; 94, Lady Worsley by Reynolds, Sir Joshua, Harewood House, Yorkshire, UK/BAL; 94, DeA Picture Library/ART; 95, Native American trading furs by American School/BAL; 96, Oxford Science Archive/Heritage Images/GET; 97, De Agostini/GET; 97, Joel Sartore/National Geographic Creative; 98, Vasco da Gama visiting the Rajah of Cannanore, India, from 'The Great Explorers Columbus and Vasco da Gama' by English School/BAL; 98, imageBROKER/Alamy; 99 (UP), TGC; 99 (LO), Antoine-Laurent Lavoisier and His Wife, by Marie Anne Pierrette Paulze, The Metropolitan Museum of Art/ART; 100 (LE), Kean Collection/GET; 100 (RT), Universal History Archive/GET; 101 (RT), Peter I the Great by Delaroche, Hippolyte (Paul), Hamburger Kunsthalle, Hamburg, Germany/BAL; 101 (LE), TGC; 102 (UP), Portrait of David Garrick/BAL; 102 (LO), Images of Our Lives/Hulton Archive Creative/GET; 103, AA World Travel Library/Alamy; 104, The Ridotto by Gobbis, Giuseppe, San Diego Museum of Art/BAL; 105, David Yoder/National Geographic Creative; 106 (UP), Declaration of Independence by John Trumbull/GraphicaArts/Corbis; 106 (LO), Lori Epstein/NGS; 107, Spirit of '76 by Archibald M. Willard/Corbis; 108 (UPLE), The Metropolitan Museum of Art/ART; 108 (UPRT), The Metropolitan Museum of Art/ART; 108 (LO), DenisNata/SS; 109, The Print Collector/Heritage-Images/GET; 110 (LE), Marie Antoinette after Vigee-Lebrun by Clay, Louise Campbell, Guildhall Art Gallery, City of London/BAL; 110 (RT), Apic/GET; 111 (UP), TGC; 111 (LOLE), If She Could See Me, by Eugenio Scomparini/DeAgostini/GET; 111 (LORT), Napoleon in His Study by Jacques-Louis David/The Gallery Collection/Corbis

CHAPTER 7: 112-113, Library of Congress Prints & Photographs Division; 114 (UP), Scripps College, Ella Strong Denison Library, Macpherson Collection, Costume Plates of Myrtle Tyrrell Kirby; 114 (LO), Luddites marching by English School/BAL; 115, Heritage Images/GET; 117 (UPLE), Portrait of a young boy holding a parrot by Geest, Wybrand Simonsz. de, Rafael Valls Gallery, London/BAL; 117 (UPRT), BAL/GET; 117 (LOLE), Federico Ubaldo della Rovere aged 2, by Barocci or Baroccio, Federico Fiori, Museo di Palazzo Mansi, Lucca, Italy/BAL; 117 (LORT), Louis XV as a child, 1714 by Gobert, Pierre, Prado, Madrid, Spain/BAL; 118 (UPLE), The Macdonald Children by Raeburn, Sir Henry; Upton House, Warwickshire, UK/BAL; 118 (UPRT), The Metropolitan Museum of Art/ART; 118 (LO), Portrait of Cornelia Burch aged 2 Months by Dutch School, Ferens Art Gallery, Hull Museums, UK/BAL; 119 (UP), Romualdo Alinari's children, Adele and Arturo, on stilts, Florence, by Fratelli Alinari/BAL; 119 (LO), Mary Evans Picture Library/Alamy; 120, Library of Congress Prints & Photographs Division; 121 (UP), Chaka in battle at the head of the regiment of Tulwana impi by McBride, Angus/BAL; 121 (LO), The Print Collector/Print Collector/GET; 122, The Metropolitan Museum of Art/ART; 123 (LE), Chronicle/Alamy; 123 (RT), Hulton Archive/GET; 124, Fine Art Images/Heritage Images/GET; 125 (UP), Time Life Pictures/Mansell/Time Life Pictures/GET; 125 (LO), adoc-photos/Corbis

CHAPTER 8: 126-127, Lewis Hine/Library of Congress Prints & Photographs Division; 128, Lewis Hine/Library of Congress Prints & Photographs Division; 129 (LE), public domain; 129 (RT), Hulton Archive/GET; 131, GraphicaArts/Corbis; 132 (LE), London Stereoscopic Company/GET; 132 (RT), London Stereoscopic Company/GET; 133 (UPLE), London Stereoscopic Company/GET; 133 (LO), The Metropolitan Museum of Art/ART; 134 (UP), Crinolette, by English School; Fashion Museum, Bath and North East Somerset Council/BAL; 134 (LO), Archie Miles/akg-images; 135 (LIP), TGC; 135 (CTR), ignazuri/Alamy; 135 (LO), imageBROKER/Alamy; 136, Leaving Conservatoire by Jean Beraud DeAgostini/GET; 137 (UP), The Print Collector/Print Collector/GET; 137 (LO), Library of Congress Prints & Photographs Division; 138 (LO), SMSSPL/SuperStock; 138 (UP), Scripps College, Ella Strong Denison Library, Macpherson Collection, Costume Plates of Myrtle Tyrrell Kirby; 139 (LE), Robert Estall photo agency/Alamy; 139 (RT), Jorgen Bisch/National Geographic Creative; 140, Pictorial Press Ltd/Alamy; 141 (LOLE), Library of Congress Prints & Photographs Division; 141 (UP), Underwood & Underwood/George Eastman House/GET; 141 (LORT), Hulton Archive/GET; 142, Metropolitan Museum of Art/ART; 143 (UP), Mary Evans Picture Library/Alamy; 143 (LO), Library of Congress Prints & Photographs Division; 144, Robert E Parry/National Geographic Creative; 144 (INSET), Library of Congress Prints & Photographs Division; 145, Werner Forman/Universal Images Group/GET; 146, Underwood & Underwood/Corbis; 147 (UPLE), Library of Congress Prints & Photographs Division; 147 (UPRT), MUNIR UZ ZAMAN/AFP/GET; 147 (LO), Vintage Images/GET; 148-149, Museum of the City of New York/Byron Collection/GET; 150 (UP), Harold M. Lambert/Lambert/GET; 150 (LOLE), General Photographic Agency/GET; 150 (LORT), Nina Leen//Time Life Pictures/GET; 151 (UP), H. F. Davis/Topical Press Agency/GET; 151 (LO), Antiques & Collectables/Alamy; 152 (LE), Chicago History Museum/GET; 152 (RT), Hulton Archive/GET; 153 (LE), Hulton Archive/GET; 153 (RT), Len Putnam/AP Images; 154, Hulton-Deutsch Collection/Corbis; 155 (LE), TGC; 155 (CTR), The Metropolitan Museum of Art/ART; 155 (RT), TGC; 156 (LE), DenisNata/SS; 156 (RT), The Art Archive/Kharbine-Tapabor/Jean Vigne/ART; 157 (UP), SuperStock; 157 (LO), titov dmitriy/SS

CHAPTER 9: 158-159, Siede Preis/Photographer's Choice RF/GET; 160 (INSET), Library of Congress Prints & Photographs Division; 160, Universal History Archive/UIG/GET; 161 (LO), Library of Congress Prints & Photographs Division; 161 (UP), Library of Congress Prints & Photographs Division; 162, Michael Ochs Archives/GET; 163 (UP), adoc-photos/ART; 163 (LOLE), The Metropolitan Museum of Art/ART; 163 (LORT), Neil McAllister/Alamy; 164 (INSET), Antiques & Collectables/Alamy; 164-165, AP Images; 165, Bettmann/Corbis; 166 (UP), Dave King/Dorling Kindersley/GET; 166 (LO), Angela Hampton Picture Library/Alamy; 167, Hulton-Deutsch Collection/Corbis; 168 (UP), Buyenlarge/GET; 168 (LOLE), Library of Congress Prints & Photographs Division; 168 (LORT), Fox Photos/Hulton Archive/GET; 169, Wikipedia; 170 (UP), Michael Ochs Archives/GET; 170 (CTR), R. H. Vincent/Redferns/GET; 170 (LO), MGM/Wikipedia; 171, SuperStock/GET; 172 (UP), Matt Vanderlinde/Alamy; 172 (CTR), Wikipedia; 172 (LO), Stocksnapper/SS; 173, Terence Donovan/GET; 174-175, SuperStock RM/GET; 176, Fabrice Cormy/Figarophoto/GET; 177 (UPLE), 2/Ocean/Corbis; 177 (UPRT), Vetta/GET; 177 (LOLE), Condé Nast Archive/Corbis; 177 (LORT), Anthony Barboza/GET; 178-179, Blend Images/Erik Isakson/Brand X/GET; 180 (LE), RyanJLane/E+/GET; 180 (RT), DreamPictures/GET; 181 (LE), Jose Fuste Raga/Corbis; 181 (RT), Dirk Anschutz/The Image Bank/GET

TIME LINE: 182, Ivy Close Images/Alamy; 183 (UPLE), titov dmitriy/Shutterstock; 183 (UPRT), Nina Leen/Time Life Pictures/Getty Images; 183 (LO), Chronicle/Alamy

FOR JON. —*S. A.*

PUBLISHED BY THE NATIONAL GEOGRAPHIC SOCIETY
Gary E. Knell, *President and Chief Executive Officer*
John M. Fahey, *Chairman of the Board*
Declan Moore, *Executive Vice President; President, Publishing and Travel*
Melina Gerosa Bellows, *Publisher and Chief Creative Officer, Books, Kids, and Family*

PREPARED BY THE BOOK DIVISION
Hector Sierra, *Senior Vice President and General Manager*
Nancy Laties Feresten, *Senior Vice President, Kids Publishing and Media*
Eva Absher-Schantz, *Design Director, Kids Publishing and Media*
Jay Sumner, *Director of Photography, Kids Publishing*
Jennifer Emmett, *Vice President, Editorial Director, Kids Books*
R. Gary Colbert, *Production Director*
Jennifer A. Thornton, *Director of Managing Editorial*

Staff for This Book
Jennifer Emmett, Ariane Szu-Tu, *Project Editors*
James Hiscott, Jr., *Art Director and Design*
Lori Epstein, *Senior Photo Editor*
Hillary Leo, *Photo Editor*
Paige Towler, *Editorial Assistant*
Sanjida Rashid, *Design Production Assistant*
Stuart Armstrong, *Illustrator–Time Line Graphic*
Margaret Leist, *Photo Assistant*
Grace Hill, *Associate Managing Editor*
Joan Gossett, *Production Editor*
Lewis R. Bassford, *Production Manager*
Susan Borke, *Legal and Business Affairs*

Production Services
Phillip L. Schlosser, *Senior Vice President*
Chris Brown, *Vice President, NG Book Manufacturing*
George Bounelis, *Senior Production Manager*
Nicole Elliott, *Director of Production*
Rachel Faulise, *Manager*
Robert L. Barr, *Manager*

The National Geographic Society is one of the world's largest nonprofit scientific and educational organizations. Founded in 1888 to "increase and diffuse geographic knowledge," the Society's mission is to inspire people to care about the planet. It reaches more than 400 million people worldwide each month through its official journal, *National Geographic,* and other magazines; National Geographic Channel; television documentaries; music; radio; films; books; DVDs; maps; exhibitions; live events; school publishing programs; interactive media; and merchandise. National Geographic has funded more than 10,000 scientific research, conservation, and exploration projects and supports an education program promoting geographic literacy.

For more information, please visit nationalgeographic.com, call 1-800-NGS LINE (647-5463), or write to the following address:

National Geographic Society
1145 17th Street N.W.
Washington, D.C. 20036-4688 U.S.A.

Visit us online at nationalgeographic.com/books

For librarians and teachers: ngchildrensbooks.org

More for kids from National Geographic:
kids.nationalgeographic.com

National Geographic supports K–12 educators with ELA Common Core Resources. Visit natgeoed.org/commoncore for more information.

For information about special discounts for bulk purchases, please contact National Geographic Books Special Sales:
ngspecsales@ngs.org

For rights or permissions inquiries, please contact National Geographic Books Subsidiary Rights: ngbookrights@ngs.org

Hardcover ISBN: 978-1-4263-1919-8
Reinforced library binding ISBN: 978-1-4263-1920-4

The narrative text for this book is set in ITC Giovanni. The feature text is set in Frutiger. Display heads are set in Ink Gothic Alt and Neutra Display and Text.

Printed in China

14/PPS/1